From t

Insights of a man of God

Other books by Arthur Wallis:

In the Day of Thy Power (Christian Literature Crusade)

Jesus of Nazareth: Who is He? (Christian Literature Crusade)

God's Chosen Fast (Kingsway)

Pray in the Spirit (Kingsway)

Into Battle (Kingsway)

The Radical Christian (Kingsway)

Living God's Way (Kingsway)

China Miracle (Kingsway)

On to Maturity (Kingsway)

Jesus Prayed (Christian Literature Crusade)

Arthur Wallis also made a substantial contribution to a symposium published shortly before his death:

Apostles Today, edited by David Matthew (Harvestime)

From the Prophet's Pen

Insights of a man of God

Arthur Wallis

Harvestime

Published in the United Kingdom by:
Harvestime Services Ltd, 12a North Parade, Bradford
West Yorkshire BD1 3HT

The material in this book originally appeared in
Restoration magazine
This compilation first published by Harvestime
First printed September 1989

Also quoted: Revised Standard Version (RSV), New American Standard Bible (NASB), King James Version (KJV), Revised Authorised Version (RAV), Amplified Bible (Amp)

British Library Cataloguing in Publication Data:

Wallis, Arthur 1922-1988
From the Prophet's Pen.
1. Christian life
I. Title II. Restoration
248.4

ISBN 0-947714-75-8

Typeset in the United Kingdom by:
E. Thompson (Typesetters) Ltd., Bradford BD8 7BX.
Printed and bound in the United Kingdom by:
Richard Clay Ltd., Bungay, Suffolk

Contents

Introduction

I have fond memories of Arthur Wallis.

As a teenager I remember the mixture of respect and misgiving shown towards him by delegates to a Conference of Brethren at Swanwick, Derbyshire. His gentlemanly bearing and evident godliness made him a desirable person to have around, yet his unashamed reaching out for a new experience of the Holy Spirit made many wary. When he eventually found it, their wariness gave way to rejection.

Later on, he became something of a spiritual father to me, providing encouragement and example but never shirking the task of bringing uncomfortable observations if he was convinced that's what the Lord wanted him to say. After helping him for some years in the production of *Restoration* magazine, I was honoured to succeed him as editor. His help and encouragement were unstinting.

Arthur's books have helped and inspired many, myself included. They were all prophetic, all in the vanguard of what God was saying and doing at the time. For me, *The Radical Christian* remains his best work, because of its outstandingly prophetic nature. It was not the most popular, but that is hardly to be expected of a book which challenged head-on some of Christendom's most treasured traditions.

Some, of course, would see Arthur as more a teacher than a prophet. He was indeed firm on Scripture and loved to expound its basic principles as a stimulus to Christian living. But it was his insistence on its 'here and now' relevance, its right to shape our personal and church life today, that moved him over the borderline from teacher to prophet.

And, like any true prophet, he was a man who knew God. 'If we are to be a prophetic people,' he wrote, 'there must be a God-consciousness about us. We must feel at home in his presence. Our fellowship with God must be one of reverent intimacy. You can't walk with God, spend time with God, without something of God brushing off.'

That described Arthur exactly. It was his manifest godliness that so often disarmed his critics and, hopefully, made them less inclined to reject out-of-hand his prophetic message.

It is a privilege to present to the Christian public this selection of his miscellaneous writings. All of them appeared over a period of twelve years as articles in *Restoration* magazine and are offered here with only minor editorial changes. There is no connecting theme — each essay stands on its own, making this a good book for browsing.

But be warned: the prophet, though dead, still speaks!

David Matthew
Editor

The best is yet to come

During the earlier years of my Christian life I left biblical prophecy severely alone. The experts, I argued, had been squabbling over the interpretation of coming events for centuries. Who was I to come up with any answers?

Then one day I was confronted with the fact that at least one third of the Bible is prophecy. Could I afford to adopt an attitude of indifference to so much which was written for my edification and encouragement? Were not these things hidden from the wise and prudent but revealed to babes? I felt I qualified!

Christians have tended to devalue the word 'hope', to make it little more than optimism in spiritual things. But hope is just as certain and powerful as faith itself. As the age moves on to its climax, and Satan becomes more and more desperate, we shall need to be sustained by a hope that finds a sure base in the prophetic Scriptures.

Rescued from disaster?

I was one who for many years was in great faith for things to wax worse and worse, with men both deceiving and being deceived. Wasn't that exactly what the New Testament said? I viewed the rapture of the saints (1 Thessalonians 4:16-17) as a rescue operation of a church that had failed to make it. However, I was neglecting a very important principle of prophetic interpretation.

'No prophecy of Scripture is [a matter] of any personal or private or special interpretation' (2 Peter 1:20 Amp). Whatever else the statement means, it is saying that you cannot interpret a given prophecy in isolation from other relevant prophecies. The interpretation must be in keeping with the general drift of the prophetic Scripture.

You may read certain scriptures and conclude that the world is going to get better and better until thoroughly christianised. Other passages would suggest the reverse. First we must grasp the broad sweep of God's kingdom plan.

It is not enough to 'take a sneaky look at the close of the book and find out that Jesus wins in the end'. *When* does he win? *How* does he win? Is it *in spite of us* or *because of us?* And you don't have to go to the end of the book; you'll find the answer at the beginning.

The Genesis key

It's the first prophecy of the Bible. 'I will put enmity between you [the serpent] and the woman, and between your offspring and hers; he will crush your head, and you will strike his heel' (Genesis 3:15). Here is the germ of all prophecy: a warning of conflict and a promise of ultimate victory.

First, there would be perpetual enmity between the two offsprings, representing the forces of darkness and the forces of light.

Next, the issue of the conflict would be decided when the offspring of the woman (Christ) bruised the serpent's head (Satan).

Finally, this victory would not leave the Victor unscathed. His heel would be bruised — a cryptic reference to death by crucifixion.

'The offspring of the serpent' refers to all those governed by the spirit of antichrist, people implacably opposed to the rule of Christ. Remember how Jesus said to the Pharisees, 'You belong to your father, the devil' (John 8:44)? The offspring of the serpent (those opposed to Christ) and the offspring of the woman (Christ, the Head and the body) will both come to full manifestation before the final showdown.

Though it was Christ who bruised Satan's head at the cross, it is the church who also bruises Satan's head in the final outworking of his great victory. 'The God of peace,' said Paul, 'will soon crush Satan under *your* feet' (Romans 16:20). You and I have a vital part to play. The victory of Christ is to be implemented, not in spite of the church, or apart from the church, but *through* the church.

Just as the word about the bruising of Satan's head involves us, so does the suffering of the bruised heel include us, too. It is a suffering church, one that has embraced the cross, that will triumph in the end time.

This is the picture of the victors: 'They have conquered [Satan] by the blood of the Lamb and by the word of their testimony, *for they loved not their lives even unto death'* (Revelation 12:11 RSV).

How is the kingdom to come and the final victory to be won? Three key words, which are increasingly on the lips of God's people, help us to understand what God's strategy is.

Renewal — the means, not the end

This first word has a *personal* emphasis. The charismatic renewal in the mid-1960s began with individual believers seeking the Father for his promised gift of the Holy Spirit.

Multiplied thousands all over the world have experienced the baptism in the Holy Spirit, with far-reaching results. They have received power through the on-coming of the Holy Spirit, spoken in new tongues, been set free from fears and inhibitions, and have come into a new dimension of praise, prayer and worship.

1 Corinthians 12 and 14, at one time incomprehensible, have now become clear and plain. And this for the simple reason that the wonderful gifts of the Father — tongues, interpretation, prophecy and such like — have been *experienced,* instead of being relegated to a museum of New Testament curiosities.

It is only a Spirit-baptised church that will bring in the kingdom of God. There is no bypassing the experience of renewal.

The final triumph over the powers of darkness will be accomplished by a people clothed with power and equipped with spiritual gifts. It is not enough to know about it. It is not even enough to dip a toe in the water. We must commit ourselves.

Many deeply blessed in the charismatic movement mistakenly saw it as *the end* rather than *the means*. The baptism in the Spirit became a kind of graduation certificate, and meetings where spiritual gifts operated became an end in themselves.

Then, 'Where do we go from here?' became a cry, often with no satisfactory answer. Enthusiasm began to give way to unbelief, disillusionment and even cynicism. Yet, still the movement of the Spirit rolled on, breaking new ground both at home and overseas, continuing to quicken and renew all who were hungry for God.

Restoration — an ongoing process

The second word, *restoration,* has a *corporate* emphasis. Behind it is the recognition that the power and effectiveness of the early church was not through a few dazzling individualists. Nor was it simply that all the believers had personally received the Holy Spirit, true though that was.

On the day of Pentecost a hundred and twenty men and women were not only *filled* but also *fused* into one body. That had never happened before. 'They stood on their feet a vast army.' There was no place for individualism in the early church. Community was the name of the game.

The efforts of a rowing eight or a tug-of-war team, working in perfect unison, generate much more power than the sum total of their individual efforts. So it was with the early church. It became the most powerful single element in society and a grave threat to the establishment. No wonder they were described as 'these men who have turned the world upside down' (Acts 17:6 RSV).

Can you imagine today's church ceasing to be the butt of music-hall jokes, no longer treated as a religious irrelevance, and becoming the most influential force on earth? This is God's plan and he is going to bring it to pass (see Psalm 2).

This means that we must have local churches which are not composed of both believers and those who simply profess to believe (a mix that always spells weariness), but a community of true believers, baptised in water and in the Holy Spirit, totally committed to Christ and to each other.

Here, each believer recognises that he or she has a special part to play in the functioning of the church, so that there is a building up of 'the body' to full maturity.

The unity of the early church was not simply task-orientated. Believers were not together simply because there was a job to be done. They had found each other in God. They were joined together by the Holy Spirit. They shared a common life. The world did not exclaim, 'See how zealous these Christians are for their cause,' but, 'See how these Christians love one another.'

Sprain your wrist or break your ankle, and the relationship between one part of your body and the rest is seriously impaired, the overall function detrimentally affected. Just so in the body of Christ. What a revelation it was to discover that 'church' was not really meetings and activities, but relationships. Wherever you have a breakdown of relationships, there you have a breakdown of function also.

The members are to be 'joined and held together by every supporting ligament' (Ephesians 4:16). Though we are to 'make every effort to keep the unity of the Spirit through the bond of peace' (Ephesians 4:3), what about those 'supporting ligaments'? How do they hold parts together?

Are not these the gifts of Christ that Paul had just mentioned, that is, apostles, prophets, evangelists, shepherds and teachers? Does he not say that they are God's appointed means to bring us to the unity of the faith (Ephesians 4:13)? The emphasis on restoration is bringing these gifts into their rightful place, restoring particularly those of apostles and prophets, so long denied and yet so vital for the bringing of the church to full maturity.

What exciting days these are! But to look at the situation realistically we are obliged to acknowledge ruefully that, by present standards, it is going to take thousands of years to see the kingdom triumph across the face of the earth. Many would say that any prospect of the church, so sadly segmented, coming forth as a unified army, is so unrealistic as to be an idle daydream. Even if we have faith for it, and the process speeds up, it is going to take a very long time.

But hold on. There is a weapon in God's armoury that he is still holding in reserve.

Revival — the divine break-in

Revival — there are few words in our spiritual vocabulary meaning so many different things to so many different people. On the American continent 'revival' usually describes a series of evangelistic meetings: 'We plan to have a revival in our church next month.'

Others equate it with a personal renewal as individuals are sanctified, quickened or filled with the Holy Spirit.

Many think and speak of the charismatic renewal as revival. It was the seeking of God for revival, even before the charismatic movement broke out, that led many of us into a renewal experience and to seek God concerning his will to restore his church to New Testament purity and power. But even as we came into some experience of these things we knew that revival had not yet come.

Anyone who has read widely of the true revivals of the past will have no hesitation in affirming that we have not yet seen it — at least, not in Britain.

We have certainly seen valuable movements of the Holy Spirit that have had some of the ingredients of revival, but there have been significant missing elements. I want to touch on some of these. When we see them characterising the movement of the Spirit, then we can declare that God has truly come among us in revival power.

Revival — God-consciousness

We may have been in meetings with a sweet sense of God's presence in worship, or even a powerful sense of his presence in the manifestation of healing or deliverance. But there is a visitation of God in revival that is more powerful than anything we have ever experienced.

This God-consciousness is prefigured in the Old Testament story. When Shekinah glory came down upon tabernacle and temple of old, the priests could not stand to minister. They were on their faces. A visitation of God in revival means an overshadowing of man and his activity by the overwhelming glory of God. Moses knew it when he cried out, 'I exceedingly fear and quake.'

Imagine we are in Jerusalem at Pentecost. Weeks before, the city had rung to the cry, 'Away with him, crucify him!' The populace had witnessed the fulfilment of their plea.

Then there were disturbing rumours that Jesus was alive. Then came Pentecost, and those discouraged, dispirited disciples came out into the open and boldly declared, 'The Jesus that you have crucified is alive and he is the Messiah.'

It took the city by storm. Three thousand were saved on the spot. Then we read, 'And fear came upon every soul' (Acts 2:43 RSV). Imagine that great metropolis, the centre of world Jewry, caught in the grip of God!

This feature has not been characteristic of the charismatic renewal, but it *is* characteristic of revival. Let us prepare ourselves for something grander than we have yet experienced. We shall see salvation without sermons, healing without imposition of hands, and deliverance without a commanding word.

This is not to say that God wants to do away with human instruments. He simply wishes to remind us that he is quite capable of working without them.

Revival — community impact

The charismatic renewal has now been around for years. Yet many in our churches, not to mention the vast majority of our citizens, know nothing about it. They have not been touched by it. It is clear that the community impact has been minimal.

In true revivals, community impact is a major feature. People do not have to read the *Gospel Gazette* in order to discover that God is among his people.

As well as the God-consciousness that we have been speaking about, there are signs and wonders that fill men and women with awe and wonder. The message of the kingdom becomes the major talking-point in the pubs and the clubs. There may be debating and discussing, mocking and scoffing, but indifference is no longer possible.

When people can neither deny nor explain what is happening, when indifference to the gospel is no longer possible, when sin hides its head in shame, then we will know that revival has truly come.

Revival — conversion harvest

This is the crowning blessing of a true visitation of the Holy Spirit — a harvest for the kingdom of God. But it is more than large numbers of converts. This can happen and does happen without revival. It is the *manner* in which they are converted. It is the depth of conviction of sin, the travail with which they come and are born into the kingdom.

Remember the lame man at the Beautiful Gate? Following the arrest of the apostles, they were tried by the Sanhedrin. When they saw the man who had been healed standing with the apostle, these religious leaders could say nothing against what had happened.

The healed man did not need to align himself in this fashion. But so deep was the work of God's Spirit in him, far deeper than a physical healing, that he was eager to be identified with those who had brought him salvation.

In revival you don't need to follow the converts up; they follow you up!

We have only to read the history of revivals of the past to get some idea of how great the harvest can be. The task of world evangelism, the establishing of the rule of Christ throughout the earth, and the full restoration of the church to be 'fair as the moon, clear as the sun, and terrible as an army with banners', can never be accomplished apart from such visitations of the Holy Spirit.

Get ready — it's coming!

There's no question about it, the best is yet to be! Many promises of such a visitation, given by God to his people over the years, have not yet been fulfilled. Again and again God has spoken in prophecy of an outpouring of his Spirit which can only be described as God doing 'immeasurably more than all we ask or imagine, according to his power that is at work within us'.

Is it then a sovereign act of God for which we must patiently wait? Must we simply twiddle our thumbs till God's zero hour strikes?

No, indeed. We have our part to play. There are conditions that we need to fulfil. They do not rate as revival, nor do they ensure that it will come. It is rather that God informs us that revival is coming, and then commands us to get ready for it.

'If my people, who are called by my name, will *humble themselves* and *pray* and *seek my face* and *turn from their wicked ways,* then will I hear from heaven and will forgive their sin and will heal their land' (2 Chronicles 7:14).

How desperately our land needs healing! Only revival can accomplish it.

Let us respond with all our hearts to these four things that God requires of us, and become a people willing and ready for the coming day of his power.

A prophetic people

It becomes increasingly evident with every passing year that the Big Powers are no longer in charge of world events (if they ever were). World events are in charge of them.

The situation resembles a giant petrol-tanker careering at ever-increasing speed down a long steep hill, while the driver fights desperately but fruitlessly to regain control. We alone, as God's people, have cause for optimism. We see a light on the horizon which grows brighter as the world's darkness deepens.

We hold in our hand a *prophetic Book,* which is not only 'a lamp to [our] feet' to show us the next step, but also 'a light for [our] path' shining far down the road. The prophetic Word is to prevent us being caught unawares by end-time events. It will give us security and hope if we 'pay attention to it, as to a light shining in a dark place, until the day dawns' (2 Peter 1:19).

We have also a *prophetic Guide,* even 'the Spirit of truth', sent by God to guide us into all the truth and 'to tell us what is yet to come'. By itself the Book would be of no more use to us than a map to a blind man. He needs a guide, and so do we. What comfort and security to know that the Author of the prophetic Scriptures is with us to interpret them to us!

As for ourselves, we are a *prophetic people.* 'All the prophets from Samuel on . . . have foretold these days. And you are heirs of the prophets' (Acts 3:24-25). In other words, 'You are a prophetic people living in a prophetic day.'

If that was true when Peter spoke those words, how much more today. We are the people 'on whom the fulfilment of the ages has come' (1 Corinthians 10:11).

A prophetic community is not one with its head in the clouds, passively waiting for the end of all things. Spurgeon chided the early Brethren movement for its preoccupation with the Lord's return: 'Ye men of Plymouth,' he wrote, 'why stand ye gazing up into heaven? Get on with your work!'

The prophet of old had both feet firmly on the ground. He spoke a relevant word to the situation. As a prophetic people we, too, speak a 'now word' to our generation, and demonstrate it by what we are.

But we can only be 'a people of today' by being also 'a people of tomorrow'. We hold our heads erect, square our shoulders to the world, and look undismayed at the darkening clouds only because we are a people with a heavenly destiny. We know we are winning through, and that we shall stand at last with our great Captain, victorious on the field of battle.

Righteousness — the unchanging principle

Though politics is defined as 'the science and art of government', it is also used to describe that which is scheming, artful or cunning. In speaking of our enemies, our national anthem calls on God to 'Confound their politics, Frustrate their knavish tricks, God save the Queen'!

People are cautious, if not positively distrustful, of politics. The man in the street is shrewd enough to know that the politician is only a human being like himself, and therefore subject to the same selfish motivations and sectional interests, despite all his protestations of acting for 'the good of the nation as a whole'. The simple fact is human government fails to be characterised by righteousness, because of the corruption of the human heart.

And yet, despite man's scepticism about the Utopia that the politician promises is just round the corner, there is something in him that longs for a new order, for a society free from greed and graft, hatred and violence, oppression and injustice, poverty and suffering. In a word, he longs for a kingdom based on a rule of righteousness.

Only the kingdom of God provides an answer to this cry of the human heart, for 'righteousness and justice are the foundation of his throne' (Psalm 97:2). And although the final banishing of these evils that mark the rule of man will be realised only when the kingdom of God is fully established in the coming age, even now heaven's righteous government is becoming effective in individual lives and communities, and will yet become the most influential force in the earth.

'The kingdom of God does not mean food and drink but righteousness and peace and joy in the Holy Spirit' (Romans 14:17 RSV). What Paul is saying is that because God is utterly righteous his rule (or kingdom) is inevitably one of righteousness, and that brings peace and joy in its train.

Here, then, is an acid test that we may always apply to any 'spiritual' kingdom we see arising. Not, 'Does it use Scripture to support its tenets or its practices?' Not even, 'Is it marked by evidences of the supernatural, by signs and wonders?' But, 'Is it characterised by righteousness?'

If there is a lack of true openness and honesty, a hiding of what is really being taught and practised, a lack of integrity over money, a lowering of moral standards under a cloak of 'liberty', then there may well be a kingdom arising, but it will not be the kingdom of God.

Satan's strategy

Satan fears righteousness. He is filled with dread when he sees the army of the Lord 'with the weapons of righteousness for the right hand and for the left'. He knows that their arrows will be 'sharp in the heart of the king's enemies', and so he uses every means at his disposal to blunt the attack.

He may do this by minimising the importance of righteousness in the eyes of God's people, or by clouding the issue, so that people are hazy as to what righteousness really is.

A century ago Satan's attack was centred on the authenticity of God's Word. The flood of higher criticism that broke over the theological world left people asking, 'Has God said? Is this really his Word?'

This in turn led to a questioning of the value and importance of theology — the great themes of which the Bible treats, which are the foundation of our faith. Why bother your head about Christ's virgin birth or his bodily resurrection? Who can find the answers to such metaphysical questions? The important thing is ethics, how you act and behave, especially towards your neighbour. This is surely safer ground.

This is what men and women were saying in the earlier part of the century, up to World War Two. But at that time, as William Barclay has pointed out, 'No-one ever really questioned the Christian ethic . . . . No-one ever doubted that divorce was disgraceful; that illegitimate babies were a disaster; that chastity was a good thing; that an honest day's work was part of the duty of any respectable and responsible man.'

So different is the situation now that those who are younger may find it difficult to believe that it was really like that so recently. The biblical standards of Christian morality are now being relentlessly undermined. How can we know what is right and wrong? Are there any absolutes anyway? Surely such concepts as truth, goodness and honesty are relative terms? As for chastity, that's been outmoded by modern sexual liberation. There are no blacks and whites in this ethical colour scheme, just different shades of grey.

God hates mixture

On the first day of creation, having commanded light to come, 'God separated the light from the darkness.' He could not tolerate a mixture.

He taught the same principle in the law: 'You shall not let your cattle breed with a different kind; you shall not sow your field with two kinds of seed; nor shall there come upon you a garment of cloth made of two kinds of stuff' (Leviticus 19:19 RSV). Again, 'You shall not plough with an ox and an ass together' (Deuteronomy 22:10 RSV).

It was not aesthetics that God was teaching his people, but ethics. They must learn that God's rule will bring God's order, and God's order necessitates separating those things that are irreconcilably different.

That last prohibition regarding yoking an ox with an ass is given a spiritual application in the New Testament. 'Do not be yoked together with unbelievers. For what do righteousness and wickedness have in common? Or what fellowship can light have with darkness? What harmony is there between Christ and Belial? What does a believer have in common with an unbeliever?' (2 Corinthians 6:14-15).

It was said of God's Son, 'Thou hast loved righteousness and hated wickedness.' How can we be like him if the clear line of demarcation between these two qualities is lost? If we allow the righteousness of the kingdom to be diluted by unrighteousness, the kingdom loses its primary and distinctive feature. Its authority is undermined. Its cutting edge is gone. Little wonder Satan's permanent prescription is, 'The mixture as before'.

In a day when Israel was suffering from a moral landslide God said through Isaiah, 'Woe to those who call evil good and good evil, who put darkness for light and light for darkness, who put bitter for sweet and sweet for bitter!'

Let us look at some modern ethical trends and see how this is happening today.

Situation ethics

In 1966 an American professor, Joseph Fletcher, wrote what has been described as one of the most influential books of this century. It was called *Situation Ethics.*

His basic principle was that nothing is intrinsically or universally good or bad. It depends on the circumstances. Goodness and badness are only things that happen to actions in different situations. The individual therefore must bring to every situation an act of judgment. He must decide in the light of circumstances what is right or wrong.

The only standard, he maintained, is that of love. Love is the only thing that is absolutely and universally good. And by love is meant that inflexible determination to seek the highest good of the one loved.

In Vancouver I met a Dutch couple who were serving the Lord in the Northwest Territories of Canada. The wife told me how, during the last war when Holland was occupied by the Nazis, her family had sheltered Jews and other people on the wanted list. She was only sixteen when, in the street one day, she found a gun at her chest and a group of German soldiers questioning her as to who was being hidden in the house.

Although she was then a committed Christian she lied, and those seeking refuge in her house were not discovered. Was she right or wrong? This is the kind of problem 'situation ethics' poses.

We cannot get our thinking clear here unless we have the right point of reference. Morality cannot be viewed apart from God. 'Why do you call me good?' asked Jesus of the rich young man. 'No-one is good but God alone.'

Jesus was not denying his deity. In a veiled kind of way he was asserting it. What he was implying was this: 'Why do you address me as a mere human teacher, and yet call me good. If I'm good then I'm God. And if you can't recognise me as God, then don't call me good.'

'God is light, and in him is no darkness at all.' God alone is the source of all good. Man cannot be righteous or act righteously except in relationship with God. On this basis what may appear to human judgment a fine and noble act may be either worthless or positively evil in the estimate of God.

So often the reasoning behind these ethical problems seems to take no account of an all-wise, all-powerful, all-loving God who rules the affairs of men and women. There are matters even more important than the preservation of physical life. One can see the faulty premise on which justification for abortion or euthanasia is often argued. When man is being urged to exercise his moral judgment in such situations, he is in fact being tempted to seize the reins of government from the hands of God.

Some guiding principles

'To the corrupt and unbelieving nothing is pure' — everything is relative — because 'their minds and consciences are corrupted' (Titus 1:15). Sin has distorted man's moral judgment. His only guide is probably a defiled, dulled and uninstructed conscience.

But once he is born of the Spirit, his conscience is cleansed, his mind renewed, and he begins to grow up into maturity where his faculties will be 'trained by practice to distinguish good from evil'. But how is this done?

'You are wrong, because you know neither the Scriptures nor the power of God.' That's how Jesus answered the liberals of his day, and how, I fancy, he would answer their modern counterparts.

Here, then, is our first principle. As believers we are to know the Scriptures and submit to them. We do not admit for one moment that there are no absolutes, and that God has not made his mind clear on vital issues but left things to our discretion according to circumstances.

We should view that young Dutch girl's agonising dilemma with the utmost compassion. In her position we might well have done the same. But this should not cloud the issue. 'To God, the Lord, belongs escape from death' (Psalm 68:20 RSV). We are not required to try to effect by unrighteous means what we fear he may be unwilling to do.

Lying, cheating, deceiving, stealing, committing fornication or adultery, taking another's life, whether an unborn baby or someone in the throes of a terminal illness, will *never* be justified by one who is 'captive to the Word', for the Word is surely clear on these issues.

'You know neither the Scriptures nor the *power of God.'* Here is the second guiding principle. 'God reigns.' He has not abdicated. He is still in charge. He is all-powerful. 'He does according to his will' in heaven and on earth.

And that means *now,* not just in some future golden age. It is a false principle that the end (however good and noble it may appear) justifies the means (even though these are unrighteous). The fact is that where a man submits in heart to the rule of God, the means will be wholly in keeping with the righteous end, for that is the characteristic of the rule of God.

What about Rahab, who is described as a 'justified' person? Did she not lie, and thus save the lives of the two spies? True, and there are many similar biblical examples. God *permits* many things that are not righteous and uses them to his own ends, like the works of Satan, or 'the wrath of man', but he does not thereby *authorise* them.

And because God uses sinful men and sinful acts, he is not shut up to these. If God had foreknown that Rahab would tell the truth, could he not have overruled to avert the situation? Whenever we act in submission to the will and Word of God we may safely leave the consequences with him. They are his responsibility.

As we walk in the fear of the Lord and in the light of his Word, we shall see with increasing clarity the thing that is good and right in his sight. But more than this, we have been brought under the immediate and direct rule of the King. So long as we submit in heart to that rule we are led by his Spirit.

The new covenant has not simply provided a higher set of rules than under the old, but a new life principle: 'I will put my Spirit within you, and cause you to walk in my statutes.' God has made every provision for us to know and do his will. That is kingdom living, marked by 'righteousness and peace and joy in the Holy Spirit'.

Attitudes are all-important

The church was not lacking a New Testament structure. It was led by a team of elders assisted by deacons. They sang the latest Scripture songs. They raised and clapped their hands. Occasionally — very occasionally — one or two of the extroverts would break forth into a dance before the Lord.

The teaching was biblical and well-laced with kingdom jargon. It was a water-baptised and Spirit-baptised community. The week-night meetings were in homegroups under their leaders. Other Christians looked upon them as an avant-garde charismatic church.

Yet you only had to be with them for a short time to sense that there was something not quite right. So let us look at this church a little more closely to see if we can learn what is wrong.

Though the worship has many elements that we might associate with the liberty of the Spirit, there is in fact little real liberty. The worship does not flow freely. There is a manifest absence of that essential ingredient of freedom in the Spirit: a sense of the presence of God. We do not find it a heartwarming experience to worship with this company, and we have a suspicion that they themselves are not finding it heartwarming either.

The proceedings seem to lack sparkle, freshness and variety. There is no sense of eager anticipation of what God might have in store. In fact, the expression on some faces seems to say, 'We've heard it all before.' They are evidently only expecting the usual, and consequently that is all they are getting.

As they sing their songs, there are few faces exuding the joy of the Lord. Even fewer that are lost in God. Though all are free to bring their priestly offerings of thanksgiving or prayer to God, few in fact do so. The burden of keeping the meeting moving — and a burden it clearly is — rests heavily on the leaders.

It is no surprise to learn that the few additions to the church in the past year have been the result of relocation of saints rather than regeneration of sinners.

As we spend time with these believers, and have fellowship with them outside of meetings, observing how they relate to one another in real life, we begin to see what their real need is.

Here are believers who genuinely love the Lord, and in most cases are desirous of going on with God. They have clearly found God, but have not somehow found each other. Many of them are making progress individually, but the body is not making progress together.

Their relating is at a superficial level. They are a Christian community only in name. They clearly view themselves as Christ's 'body' in their locality, but they are not like the body referred to in Ephesians 4:16, whose members are 'joined and knit together'.

Relationships are the very essence of church life, and if these are not healthy and strong, that body of Christians will never function effectively for God.

We should expect that a church truly planted by God will not only grow up but grow together. If this growing is arrested or stunted, we must not dismiss this misfortune as 'one of those things'. There is always a spiritual cause that may be identified and rectified. Somewhere, spiritual principles are being neglected or violated.

'Surfaces to be joined must be clean, dry and free of grease.' We have often read these words on a tube of adhesive. Scripture speaks of believers being *'joined'* to the Lord and *'joined'* to one another. The Greek word *(kollao)* has the primary meaning of 'glued together', which emphasises the strength of relationship that is envisaged here.

So it is important that spiritual surfaces to be joined together be 'clean and dry'. What do we mean?

Watch your spirit

'I would rather have a man who was wrong in his judgment but right in his spirit, than a man who was right in his judgment but wrong in his spirit.' This saying, attributed to Watchman Nee, emphasises the supreme importance of our attitude or spirit.

Malachi delivered his message to God's people at the close of the Old Testament age. The situation then was not dissimilar to that which we face as we move towards the close of this age. There was a serious breakdown of family relationships, as evidenced by the alarming rise in the divorce rate (2:13-16) and the generation gap (4:6). Worshippers were weeping and mourning when they came before God because they knew that he was not accepting their offerings.

From the time of Cain and Abel, God has had a way of letting people know when their offerings were accepted. Even today we know when he accepts our worship because he graces the meeting with his presence. We know that he responds to our offerings of prayer when he grants us the things that we ask.

God told Israel through Malachi that their tears on his altar would not produce a response from him because there were things that must be put right. There was a grievous relationship problem: marriages were breaking up as husbands divorced their wives.

We have to learn that under the new covenant a bad marriage relationship will detrimentally affect the prayer life of those concerned. 'Husbands . . . be considerate as you live with your wives, and treat them with respect . . . so that nothing will hinder your prayers' (1 Peter 3:7).

Having expressed through Malachi his hatred of divorce and violence, all-too-prevalent features of our modern society, God put his finger on the root of the problem. What they needed to watch was their attitude, their spirit: *'Guard yourself in your spirit'* (Malachi 2:15).

This passage in Malachi teaches us that when there is a breakdown in relationship (and marriage is the most basic human relationship of all), it is to our spirit or attitude that we need to look.

Elsewhere in Scripture we learn that our relationship with one another is always a reflection of our relationship with God. Loving God and loving my brother are inextricably bound together. If I think I can be in close communion with God and out-of-sorts with my brother, I am deluded (1 John 3:14, 17; 4:20-21).

Help! I'm hurt!

In the rough-and-tumble of human relationships it is inevitable that from time to time we all get hurt. Someone may have acted thoughtlessly or insensitively. Unwise or unkind words may have been spoken.

Such hurts need not, indeed should not, result in a *wounded* spirit, yet many are suffering from this spiritual malaise in our Christian communities and consequently they are unable to relate to their brothers and sisters.

One feels that he is not being recognised and made room for. Another feels that she is not appreciated or commended for the things she does. Yet another that his views were not consulted or his feelings considered in some decision made or action taken. Yet another is hurt because someone else has been given a position of leadership that he thought was coming to him.

Nature has made provision for the remedying of physical wounds by a built-in healing mechanism. Broken bones knit together again, cuts and bruises begin to heal. If the body does not perform this kind of self-healing operation, either it must be in a sickly state or the wound has become infected.

It is similar in the spiritual realm. We expect wounds to come, but we also expect them to heal — unless they become infected by unforgiveness, resentment and self-pity.

The wound that is festering with these things is not only failing to heal but is injecting its poison into the spiritual body, adversely affecting other believers. 'See to it that . . . no bitter root grows up to cause trouble *and defile many*' (Hebrews 12:15).

Some, when wounded, behave like a wounded dog, even biting the hand that seeks to help. Others withdraw into their shells and become uncommunicative and unco-operative. There are many in our churches whose spirit is crying out, 'I'm hurt. Who's going to do something about it?'

The answer is, 'You yourself are the one to do something about it, because God holds you responsible for your attitude.'

'But you don't know how that sister has treated me.'

No, but God does, and he still commands you to take heed to your spirit.

Even if the action that caused the hurt was as wrong as the aggrieved person makes it out to be (and this is seldom the case), his reaction is just as wrong.

I was speaking to a young couple who were clearly very hurt by some action taken by the leadership of their church. 'What is it inside you that is hurting?' I asked. 'Is it the "new man" or is it the "old man"?'

The silence that followed my question made it clear that they recognised that the 'new man' could not be hurt in this way, and that the 'old man' had no business to be around, for God had told them to put him off long ago.

The moment we recognise that the spirit we are displaying is not a Christ-like spirit, that it is wrong, that it really springs from uncrucified flesh, we have taken the first vital steps towards the healing of the wound.

We never get through so long as we persist in justifying our attitude on the basis of somebody else's wrong. The wound will only be cleansed and healed when we repent before God of our wrong attitude and take full responsibility for it. Then it is that the healing love of God comes pouring in, and if we have been wronged, our previous unforgiving spirit is replaced by a prayer for those who have wrongly used us, just as Jesus commanded.

Just look at him!

Equally as destructive of any close-knit relationship is a *judgmental* spirit.

Jesus spoke of judging in two quite distinct ways. One kind of judging he clearly forbade: 'Judge not, that you be not judged.' The other kind he commended: 'Stop judging by mere appearances, and make a right judgment' (John 7:24).

It is essential that I judge my brother's actions in the sense of assessing whether they are right or wrong, otherwise how can I follow what is good and avoid what is evil? The mature are described as those 'who by constant use have trained themselves to distinguish good from evil' (Hebrews 5:14). That means *judging,* and we are having to do this all the time.

What Christ forbade was 'playing the judge' or sitting in judgment upon others. As a judge listens to a case in court he is forming an opinion, but not until all the evidence has been presented will he pass judgment. The sin of criticism is that we pass sentence on a brother on the basis of partial evidence.

We are not in possession of all the facts. We cannot read the motives of the person's heart, and without that we cannot evaluate his actions. Hence, 'Judge nothing before the appointed time; wait till the Lord comes. He will bring to light what is hidden in darkness and will expose the motives of men's hearts' (1 Corinthians 4:5).

The critic is guilty most of all of the sin of presumption. He is assuming a role for which he is not qualified and to which God has not appointed him. 'Brothers, do not slander one another. Anyone who speaks against his brother or judges him speaks against the law and judges it. When you judge the law, you are not keeping it, but sitting in judgment on it. There is only one Lawgiver and Judge, the one who is able to save and destroy. But you — who are you to judge your neighbour?' (James 4:11-12).

We may label our package of criticism 'fair comment'. We may try to disguise it with a spiritual wrapper by prefacing it with some mildly positive remark: 'In many ways he's a very good brother, *but* . . . .' Or, 'I'm sure the sister means well, *but* . . . .' This little ploy does not deceive God nor make our critical utterance any more acceptable.

The passing of a judgment springs from a judgmental spirit, whose roving eyes are watching for some opportunity to express itself. Very often *pride* lies at the heart of this attitude. It is not that we are simply motivated by the desire to put someone else down, but that we are taking advantage of the opportunity to lift ourselves up.

If I say, 'I just can't stand that brother's arrogance,' I am wanting you to understand that I would never be arrogant like that. In fact, I am very humble, though of course I would be the last person to say so! Such expressions of a critical spirit are nothing but a thinly-veiled exercise in self-exaltation at the expense of somebody else.

Often this attitude is directed against those in leadership:

'I don't like the way he runs the housegroup.'

'If he's meant to be an elder, I don't think much of his teaching.'

'I think the elders have made a big mistake in altering the time of the Sunday meeting.'

This is the most serious form of a judgmental spirit, for those whom God has set over us are his delegated authority. At the root of this criticism is rebellion. In the book of Numbers we have repeated examples of the people grumbling against Moses and Aaron, and God viewed this as rebellion against himself.

Moses was not faultless in his leadership, of course, but God had invested him with authority, and when that was challenged God always vindicated it. 'Do not touch my anointed ones; do my prophets no harm' is a word that we must always heed.

Other forms of negative speaking are more of the nature of gossip. There are those who find some inward satisfaction in retailing the failures of others. That bit of gossip is like a tasty morsel which feeds the carnal nature within.

But whatever the form and whatever the motivation, a judgmental attitude is all too common among God's people. It destroys sound relationships. If your conscience smites you here, ask God to expose the root and then determine to deal with it ruthlessly at the cross. (For more on this 'judgment' theme, see 'This business of judging'.)

I can't trust people

In every church we find people who fail to be truly knitted and joined with their brothers and sisters because their attitude is one of *mistrust.*

Sometimes this stems from an experience of being badly let down in the past, like the case of the lady who opened her heart confidentially to someone, only to find that her trust had been betrayed, and garbled versions of what she had said came from various quarters. Now she has great difficulty in trusting anyone.

This kind of person finds it very difficult to accept anything at its face value. There is always a searching for ulterior motives behind what people say or do, so that situations are often misunderstood or misread. Such people are usually supersensitive and everybody has to tread warily to avoid stepping on their corns. They easily feel 'got at' or discriminated against.

With others a spirit of mistrust is displayed by shyness, timidity, fear of exposure, feelings of insecurity, and consequently reluctance to open up their lives to others.

'I couldn't join that lot,' said a Christian lady about a church I was involved with; 'they'd find out what kind of person I am.' It is obvious that no strong and healthy relationships can be formed until those concerned are delivered from such an attitude of mistrust.

Mistrust has its root in *fear.* Again, the way of deliverance begins by accepting responsibility for a wrong attitude, rather than blaming that 'bad experience' or the deeply suspicious nature I inherited from Grandma.

Christ's death on the cross was not only to deliver us from our sin, but also from our fear (Hebrews 2:14-15). By faith we can 'cash in' on this part of our spiritual inheritance.

We may not know where that spirit of timidity came from, but we can be sure it did *not* come from God. 'God did not give us a spirit of timidity, but a spirit of power, of love and of self-discipline' (2 Timothy 1:7). By faith I can loose myself from my bond of captivity.

Once free, you will be able to share with your brothers and sisters what God has done for you, and that will be the first vital step in opening up yourself to them. Now that the fear has gone, you will find yourself able to receive their love at its face value, and to discover to your surprise that they are wholly *for* you. It will be God's love, flowing through them, that will complete the healing.

We have been placed in the body of Christ, each with a unique role to play. But the body of Christ is so constituted that we cannot fulfil that adequately without our brothers and sisters. We can only function effectively and fruitfully out of relationship. A dislocated shoulder means an arm that is non-functional.

The New Testament has so much to say about relationships in the body of Christ because relationships are so important. They will never come right without right attitudes. As we take heed to our spirit God will see to it that strong and healthy relationships are forged, enabling us to function in security and fruitfulness.

Kingdom now

'The kingdom now or the kingdom yet to come?' The theologians had been arguing about it for ages and believers were generally unclear about it when the charismatic renewal hit Britain in the 1960s.

Because the new birth is the entry to both church and kingdom, many assumed that the ideas were synonymous. Others thought 'kingdom' must refer to a future millennial reign of Christ on earth. But most had no clear idea at all.

Although dispensational teaching had had its origins in Britain, it had never caught on here as strongly as it had in the USA. Nevertheless, many had been unconsciously influenced by it. According to this prophetic view, the church was sentenced to decline and doomed to failure till Christ returned. The glorious finale of a triumphant church brought about by his return was thus viewed as its only hope of avoiding extinction.

The contradictions and inconsistencies in this teaching were highlighted by the new movement of the Holy Spirit.

'The works that I do shall [you] do also; and greater works . . .' (John 14:12 NASB). How could the picture of a forlorn and beleaguered church with its back to the wall, waiting for evacuation, be squared with this promise of Christ? Were we not called to take dominion over the works of darkness as had that dynamic church of the New Testament?

God began to highlight certain scriptures to confirm this view of a triumphant church. There were the Old Testament predictions of Christ's ascension ministry that were to give us Pentecost and the promised end-time outpouring of the Holy Spirit.

For example, there was God's declaration, 'I have installed my King on Zion, my holy hill,' followed by his promise to that King, 'I will make the nations your inheritance, the ends of the earth your possession' (Psalm 2:6, 8). Or those words, 'Sit at my right hand until I make your enemies a footstool for your feet' (Psalm 110:1).

A dramatic change was to take place in the status of Christ's enemies, a change that hadn't happened when he was invited to sit but would happen before he was commanded to return. It pointed to a mighty triumph over the enemies of Christ *in this age.*

This conviction has provided a needed prophetic impetus in evangelism. The church has been given authority to bring in the kingdom by saving the lost, delivering the captives, healing the sick and building up the body of Christ.

The growing response is only the firstfruits. Along with it has come a new emphasis on a kingdom lifestyle in marriage and family life, in social and moral issues and in business and work ethics.

The church is limbering up, not to splutter out like a spent candle but to exit to the coming age in a blaze of glory.

Meeting with God

Among a number of Scripture plaques for sale on the display table my eye alighted on an open 'Bible' carved from two blocks of wood and hinged together. One 'page' had the famous 'praying hands' carved on it, and the other the promise God gave to Moses, 'I will meet with thee' (Exodus 25:22 KJV).

The words touched a chord in my heart, and I secretly decided that before I left this Christian community in southern Spain I would buy that wooden Bible. But I didn't need to; on the last night they presented it to me. It faces me now in my study, a constant reminder of God's willingness to meet with those who hunger for him. Does anyone know of a greater thrill or a higher privilege to be experienced on earth?

As I look back over the forty years and more since I knew the call of God, meeting with him has not consistently been my experience. At times I have got my priorities wrong and have allowed the pressures of life to crowd out those times.

Much more frequently I have made time for my devotional life, but it could only be described as 'pedestrian' — the Word has been dry and my prayers uninspired. One thing is certain: I have learnt some important lessons, and these I want to share.

Spontaneity or discipline?

Spontaneity is a mark of the Holy Spirit. When he comes to us he demonstrates it in the way he inspires us to worship and exercise our spiritual gifts. 'The wind blows where it pleases . . . . So it is with everyone born of the Spirit.'

On this basis it would be easy to conclude that our times of meeting with God should be quite unpremeditated and spontaneous. We would have such times when we felt like it, or when the Spirit inspired us to do so. This view, however, leaves out a vital factor.

While not ruling out the element of spontaneity and the importance of being always ready to respond to the sudden urge of the Spirit, the lives of the great saints as well as the clear teaching of the Bible confirm that our life with God will always be shallow, immature and inconsistent if we do not couple spontaneity with discipline. It is not either/or but both. The man who achieved the unique distinction of walking with God for three hundred years, Enoch, boasts a name that is derived, significantly enough, from a Hebrew root meaning 'dedicated, trained and disciplined'.

In practical terms, self-discipline means that we must make up our minds to distinguish clearly between *the urgent,* ever clamouring for our attention regardless of any other claim, and *the important,* to which we must always give priority.

Self-discipline means repeatedly saying 'No' to self-will and self-pleasing in order to give God first place. An undisciplined believer is invariably self-centred, and that will show up even in the way he tries to serve God. What God wants us to do for him and what we want to do for God are not necessarily the same. As under the old covenant priesthood, so for the believer-priest today, there has to be a purging even in regard to 'the Lord's holy things' (Leviticus 5:15) and 'the sacred gifts' we offer to him (Exodus 28:38).

The 'one thing needful'

In seeking times with God which are fruitful and fulfilling I have learned that self-discipline is not the starting-point. If the stream is not flowing fully it is not the stream-bed but the spring that you must first examine. The most common cause of neglect, inconsistency or lifeless routine is *lack of spiritual hunger.*

That is easily stated but not so easily remedied. We know that Jesus said, 'Blessed are those who hunger and thirst . . . .' What we don't often know is why we fail to do just that.

The reasons may be deep and complex, beyond our ability to fathom. We need to seek the Searcher of hearts with the prayer, 'Teach me what I cannot see' (Job 34:32). God always responds to a sincere prayer of this kind, but he doesn't always show us everything at once. That would probably overwhelm us. He knows how much we can take at a time, and as we take the first step of adjustment there is an immediate increase in the flow of the Spirit. But we must persevere and see the whole thing through if we are to know the fullest blessing in our times with God.

Hunger for God is one of the most reliable barometers of our real relationship with him. When the phone was installed in our new home there was a fault in the underground cable. With the help of a special detector they traced it to a point right in front of our house. The cable had not been properly sunk, and the builders had lit a bonfire right on the spot.

The Holy Spirit who searches the deep things is the detector who enables us to pin-point the cause of our lack of hunger, then helps us to deal with it.

Variety — the spice of life

In the evangelical circles in which I was reared there was great emphasis on 'The Quiet Time', as the daily time set aside for Bible reading and prayer was usually called. The depression I sometimes experienced when I missed that time, feeling that the day was doomed to defeat and failure, was only matched by my perplexity on other occasions when, having religiously observed it, I had a day of failure just the same!

I had to learn the simple lesson that victory comes by relying on God, not on a 'Quiet Time'. It was not that the teaching was necessarily legalistic, but that my response was legalistic.

Now I no longer have a regular '*Quiet* Time', though I do have a regular time with God. What I mean is that the term is now a misnomer. When there is no danger of anyone thinking that I am making an affray, creating public disorder or otherwise disturbing the household, I can be quite noisy when I meet with God! I may sing, clap, dance or even shout. I may laugh or weep.

Why shouldn't I be noisy? I am a probationer for heaven, and if the book of Revelation is anything to judge by, that is a very noisy place. David belonged to the old covenant, but even he found going to the altar of God was his 'exceeding joy'. Surely it shouldn't be anything less under the new.

My wife and I are as deeply in love today as we were when we got married over thirty years ago. When I return home after being away for several days it is a time of animated conversation. There is so much to share, and, like most women, my wife wants 'the small print'.

There are other times when we 'let our hair down', to use a somewhat inappropriate figure of speech. We can romp and rag, laugh and tease, just like a pair of kids. 'What! At your age?' someone will ask. Well, how old was Isaac when king Abimelech, peeping through the window, spotted him 'sporting with Rebekah his wife' (Genesis 26:8 KJV)? About ninety years old, I reckon!

At other times we can enjoy each other's company in complete silence, when surveying God's marvellous handiwork as we go hiking up in the Yorkshire Dales, or as we sit together holding hands on the sofa with soft music in the background.

In the same way our meeting with God should be marked by beautiful variety. It doesn't have to have any special ingredient, any special mix or any special order to be valid. I find great value in waiting on God in silence. This is a time of adjusting my spirit to his, a sort of tuning time — tuning out all that may have been filling my mind, and tuning in to hear distinctly anything God may want to say to me.

There are times that are marked by a silence of another kind — rare moments when I am awed into silence as I contemplate his utter purity, his unspeakable love or his amazing grace. This is the silence of wonder and adoration, when words seem superfluous or totally inadequate, and only tongues can express what would be otherwise inexpressible.

The other day I broke out in praise and thanksgiving as God reminded me of some things he had said to me in prophecy nearly twenty years ago, and which I realised he was just beginning to fulfil.

While thanking God for all that he is teaching us in the realm of praise, our corporate experience of this would scale greater heights if we each developed this art more diligently in our times alone with God. And remember, if circumstances prevent your having a noisy time outwardly, you can always have a noisy time on the inside!

The Holy Spirit helps

When it comes to reading and meditating on God's Word, I find that my approach and attitude is crucial. This is no mere intellectual exercise, no performing of a necessary chore, not even a time for getting a word for others.

I constantly remind myself that I am meeting God. He is speaking to me through his Word. What is he wanting to say to me? I am eager to know. What joy when he graciously speaks! I can identify fully with Jeremiah, who recorded, 'When your words came, I ate them; they were my joy and my heart's delight' (Jeremiah 15:16).

There is no area in which I lean more heavily on the help of the Holy Spirit than supplication and intercession. I find it good to devote a session to this ministry. I encourage myself with the thought that God invites me to draw near. He loves to hear me pray, especially for others. 'My heart is wide open to you,' he seems to say. 'Come with boldness to my throne. I want you to obtain, I want you to receive, so ask and keep on asking.'

When I have no more to say in English, or when I do not know how to pray concerning a matter, I intercede in tongues. I do not know what I am saying. I don't need to. I am praying to God, and he always knows what is the mind of the Spirit, for the Spirit always prays according to God's will (Romans 8:27).

Paul frequently exhorts us to mingle our prayers with thanksgiving — a very important aspect of intercession. This is not only because gratitude is a Christian virtue and the Spirit is grieved if we do not have a thankful spirit. It does something for our faith.

If I am praying for some specific need to be met, I recall how he has supplied in the past and thank him for his great faithfulness. I find I am praying thus with greater confidence. *Sometimes, in the midst of my asking, the Holy Spirit gives me the assurance that I am heard.* I catch the sound of the heavenly 'Amen', and find myself thanking God in advance for the answer, and that is always an exciting experience.

Must we keep repenting?

Before leaving the subject of the possible ingredients of a time with God, mention must be made of repentance and confession. Some teach that there must always be repentance, that continual brokenness is the way to keep your 'cup running over'. Years ago I read a book that took this line. Repentance, it said, was the secret of a joy-filled Christian life.

I agreed with the emphasis on humbling oneself before God, being sensitive to sin and repenting when convicted. But I do not believe that all this should be the secret of the believer's joy. Of course there is joy in receiving the grace of forgiveness, but there is greater joy in receiving the grace to live in victory. There is great relief when a bout of hiccups comes to an end, but who wants to be sentenced to recurring hiccups in order to experience the joy of relief?

Behind this emphasis there seems to lie the presupposition that recurring failure is the spiritual norm, but that is decidedly not the emphasis of the New Testament.

No-one is saying that we are *not able to sin,* but we do affirm that we are *able not to sin.* When we are living in victory, do we lose our joy because we have nothing to confess? Jesus spoke about *his* joy being in us, and of our joy therefore being full (John 15:11). Patently, the joy he constantly experienced had nothing to do with repentance and confession.

'I write this to you *so that you will not sin'*, wrote the apostle. 'But if anybody does sin, we have one who speaks to the Father in our defence' (1 John 2:1). *Not* to sin is the norm. To sin is, or should be, the exception.

It is an error to treat the emergency fire-escape as though it were the main staircase. There is a place for self-humbling, brokenness, repentance and confession, but if they are a regular feature of our own personal times with God then there is something very wrong. Remember that for every sin we commit and confess, there is grace available to register a victory rather than a defeat.

Methods must be flexible

How then should we use the time with God? George Müller of Bristol felt that intercession was work — hard work. Therefore, since we would not normally engage in hard work before we have food in our stomach, we should nourish our inner man on the Word of God before giving ourselves to intercession, and let the Word itself suggest how we pray.

Others emphasise entering God's gates with thanksgiving and his courts with praise. Adopt the method you find most helpful, but don't be rigid.

As for our reading and meditation in the Word, it is not wise to leave the choice to the inspiration of the moment. It is good to have a *plan* and to tackle some portion of the Scriptures consecutively, otherwise you may find yourself dilly-dallying in indecision.

Although I usually have something consecutive on the go, I try to keep open to the Holy Spirit for anything special he may want to open up. A 'diversion' of this sort may last for a few days, and then I get back on track again with my consecutive meditation. This gives variety.

Fix the time

'There is a time . . . for every activity under the sun' — and especially for meeting with God. It is good to fix this and try to stick to it. However, the exigencies of modern life make it vital that we be flexible on this, too.

David cried out to God at 'evening, morning and noon' (Psalm 55:17). We cannot be sure whether this was a life habit, but it does seem to have been so for Daniel: 'Three times a day he got down on his knees and prayed, giving thanks to his God, just as he had done before' (Daniel 6:10).

Factors that should affect our choice of time are these: first, it needs to be at a time least likely to be upset by variations in our schedule. Then, it needs to be when there is least likelihood of being interrupted by family demands or by those two disturbers of the peace, the doorbell and the telephone. Finally, it should be preferably when the mind is fresh and uncluttered.

Without doubt the early morning fulfils these conditions best for most of us. The self-discipline of rising early, which includes the self-discipline of getting to bed in time to do so, is in itself a valuable spiritual exercise. But mothers with a baby to feed in the early morning, or parents with little darlings who regularly burst into their bedrooms at 5.30 am, may have to choose another time until the situation changes.

'He wakens me morning by morning, wakens my ear to listen like one being taught' (Isaiah 50:4). 'But I feel like death warmed up first thing in the morning,' you say. You won't if *God* awakens you. You will be spiritually and mentally alert, and ready to receive revelation, as the prophet Zechariah was when God awakened him (Zechariah 4:1).

God is waiting

I was awake, my conscience telling me I should be getting up and my flesh reminding me how warm and comfortable bed was, when a voice inside me whispered, 'I'm waiting for you.'

The thought that God was there in my study, where I always go to meet him, awaiting my arrival with joyful expectation, was the motivation I needed. The thought that he longs to meet with me, that he created me for this, that he chose me first and foremost 'to be with him', has done the trick many times since.

Let me ask you, did you meet him when you last bowed alone in his presence or turned aside to read his Word?

You did — if your heart was freshly warmed by his love. You did — if you sensed something rising spontaneously within you in praise and thanksgiving to him. You did — if your faith was nourished and strengthened. You did — if you really touched the throne as you prayed. You did — if the simplest truths of his Word sparkled with splendour as you read them.

Remember, he is committed to meeting with you. He wants it more than you do. But you must want it, too — want it badly. He stands by his covenant promise, 'You will seek me and find me when you seek me *with all your heart*' (Jeremiah 29:13).

He is waiting.

Living at the climax

Do you know the time?

Consulting your watch will not provide the answer, but looking carefully into the Word of God in the light of what is happening around us undoubtedly will. The Jews of Jesus' day were deaf to God's 'Big Ben' booming out their hour of destiny. They did not know the time of their visitation. We do not want to make the same mistake.

So let us stop and think about time for a moment.

Time and eternity

It is impossible for us to think of time as God does, for he is an eternal Being and we are but finite creatures. He introduced himself to Moses as the great 'I AM'. Similarly, Jesus declared, 'Before Abraham was born, I am.' We are left with the impression that the Godhead lives in an eternal now.

Gigantic time-spans are as nothing to God. A thousand years are as a day, and a day as a thousand years. He inspired his apostle to write, 'The end of all things is at hand,' and then to close the record with the promise of Jesus, 'I am coming soon.' Since those words were penned, nearly two thousand years have passed, but to God that was only the day before yesterday! What are you getting impatient about?

God refuses to be bound by our neat concepts of past, present and future. He calls the things that are not as though they are, and speaks of the non-existent future as though it were the past or the present. He promises that before people call he will answer, and often assures them of victory before the battle has begun.

Understanding the ages

It is surely in condescension to our finite understanding that God divides time into successive epochs or 'ages'. There are ages past and ages to come. He knows we cannot fathom eternity and so he calls it 'the ages of the ages'.

Scripture makes it very clear that there is something very special, something quite unique, about this age of grace in which we live. It began with the great drama of redemption. To our surprise and puzzlement Hebrews tells us that this happened *'at the end of the ages'* (Hebrews 9:26). We have to understand 'end' as signifying fulfilment or consummation. It was the point of time to which all the preceding ages led up, and out of which all the proceeding ages would flow. It was *the climax* which ushered in the age of the New Testament church.

Hebrews 11 unfolds the exploits of the great heroes of faith, and then explains that they did not receive what was promised. They died in hope. For us, however, God had provided something better. It is for us to receive that for which they believed and waited in hope.

Do we realise that these giants of faith, whose exploits fill us with wondering admiration, have been *waiting for us* to come into our inheritance that they might come into theirs (Hebrews 11:39-40)? It is not them, but *'us,* on whom the fulfilment of the ages has come' (1 Corinthians 10:11).

The great climax

But there is something more. Not only is this age the climax of the ages, but as it approaches its consummation we are heading towards a climax of the climax. It is not only the Old Testament saints who have been waiting for this age, but the whole creation is now on tiptoe as it 'waits in eager expectation for the sons of God to be revealed' (Romans 8:19).

We know that this final phase will be one of great spiritual conflict. That God's people will come under enormous pressures. That there will be satanic deception. That violence and wickedness will abound. But let us be strengthened and inspired as we consider what it means to be 'living on the edge of time' at the climax of this climactic age.

Scripture focuses our attention on the beginning of this age and on its end. The age commenced with a great spiritual upheaval that overthrew the old order and took the world by storm. 'Here come the men who have turned the world upside down.' But now we are heading towards the great finale and God will see to it that it is no anticlimax.

Glorious though the church was in its inception, 'the latter splendour of this house shall be greater than the former' (Haggai

2:9 RSV), notwithstanding the appalling state of society that is predicted. The darker the night the brighter will shine the city of God.

A sense of privilege

'Many prophets and righteous men longed to see what you see but did not see it.' In these words Jesus impressed his disciples with the *privilege* that was theirs of living in what Peter later described as 'the last days' (Acts 2:17). How much greater is our privilege to be living in the last of 'the last days'.

Whether or not we live to see the final showdown, let us be inspired by the honour God has afforded us, upon whom has come the climax of this age.

A sense of destiny

As well as a sense of privilege we need to have a sense of *destiny*. We have been chosen to play a part — a special and unique part — in this closing drama of the ages.

That is how it was with Queen Esther when challenged to intervene for the deliverance of her people by entering the king's presence, unbidden, to plead on their behalf. She would be taking her life in her hands as well as risking the loss of all that she had so miraculously gained. But the words of Mordecai put steel into her spirit: 'Who knows but that you have come to royal position for such a time as this?' (Esther 4:14).

What was true of Esther is equally true of us, and for a greater cause. For this hour of destiny we were chosen. For this purpose we were born, that we might play our part in the closing drama of the ages. How vital that we know our role, and that we take heed to our ministry and fulfil it.

A sense of awe

The sense of privilege and of destiny will inevitably produce in us also a sense of *awe*. It was through Christ the Head that this age was inaugurated, and on him rested 'the spirit of the fear of the Lord'. It will be through Christ the body that the age will be consummated, so the same 'spirit of the fear of the Lord' must rest upon us.

John Bunyan reminds us that we must drop the muck-rake and lift up our eyes to the crown above our heads. It is there to be won — or lost. God is setting before us a destiny that will be the wonder of the universe.

It is time to cease play-acting and trifling. The Christian life is not a big joke. The fear of the Lord produces sobriety. 'The end of all things is near. Therefore be clear-minded and self-controlled so that you can pray' (1 Peter 4:7). Let us be people of fortitude.

May the heavenly scribe who pens the closing pages of church history record, 'This was their finest hour.'

Time — and how to redeem it

Are you always in a rush?

For ever trying to catch up? Vainly contriving to put quarts into pint pots? Seldom in rest of spirit? Often under pressure and strain? Given to wandering thoughts? So many projects begun but never finished? Tending to put off the unpleasant or difficult task? Careless and slapdash in what you do? Or demanding of yourself such perfection that your output is minimal?

If so, then Paul's exhortation about 'redeeming the time' is God's word to you (Ephesians 5:16 KJV). But, in practical terms, what does it mean?

Showing his friend round his garden, Bill pointed to the flower border and remarked piously, 'It's only the good Lord that makes 'em all grow.'

'You need to come round and see my garden,' responded his friend. 'The Almighty has had it to himself for the last four years!'

We all know that gardens don't look after themselves. If we let nature take its course the briars and brambles quickly take over and the garden is lost. It has to be constantly 'redeemed' or bought back from the dominion of the thorns and thistles that came through the curse.

When Paul speaks of 'redeeming the time' he is using a word that is otherwise only used in the New Testament of our being redeemed from the curse of the law. It means literally 'to buy out'. It implies more than 'making the most of the time' or opportunity, as modern versions render it.

If we think of the redeeming of time in much the same way as a gardener has to redeem his garden from the curse of the weeds that would take over, we will realise that it isn't a once-for-all redemption, as when the garden was first laid out and planted. It is an ongoing redemption. Neglect it and you lose it, just as surely as you lose your garden.

Another way to look at it is suggested by the parable of the pounds, where the master entrusted to each of his servants a pound and told them to trade with it until he returned. The lazy servant failed to do this with the result that he lost his pound (Luke 19:11-24).

Time is a stewardship

In that parable each servant received one pound. None received less, none more. Whether we fritter away our time or use it to the full, the fact remains that we each have exactly the same amount of it — twenty-four hours in every day.

As with the pound in the parable, it is how we handle it or mishandle it, whether we neglect it or use it, that determines whether or not we redeem it.

When Christ redeemed us, he also redeemed our time, and handed it to us, just as the master handed the pound to his servants, as a sacred trust or stewardship. Now we have to redeem it, that is, bring it fully into the good of Christ's redemption. How do we do that?

Compare time with your body. Christ's redeeming of us included our bodies, for he wanted them for himself, that through them he might express his life. But we have our part to play in this redemptive process. We have first to present our bodies *in toto* and then to set to work on the different members and present them to him as 'instruments of righteousness' (Romans 6:13). This latter is not a once-for-all affair, but an ongoing process.

In the same way, to redeem the time that God has given us means to bring this precious entrustment, in an ever-increasing measure, under the rule of Christ.

Stewardship implies both *opportunity* and *accountability,* and the stewardship of time is no exception. To each of those servants the pound represented a unique opportunity to display and develop such qualities as industry, ability, faithfulness and perseverance on behalf of his master.

But the giving of the pound was no casual affair. It wasn't given on a 'take it or leave it' basis. The master's parting words, 'Put this money to work until I come back,' clearly implied that the money was on loan, and that on his return the servant would be required to render an account of what he had done with it. To recognise that time is a stewardship is to be continually reminded that a day is coming when the Master will be asking us to render our trading account of this valuable commodity.

Spiritual arithmetic

It is Moses who gives us, in the only psalm attributed to him, our first key on how to redeem time: 'Teach us to number our days aright, that we may gain a heart of wisdom' (Psalm 90:12).

When I was a boy away at boarding school I used to 'count the days' till the end of term. I was just longing for the day when school would break up and I would go home. Then halfway through the school holidays I would again start counting the days, only very differently. I would say to myself a little wistfully, 'Only ten more days of holiday.'

Counting the days at school, I was not concerned with the present, except that it would pass as quickly as possible. My focus was entirely on the future. But at home I was counting with an emphasis on the present, to savour and to use to the full every one of those remaining days of my school vacation.

This exhortation to number our days is more to do with the second kind of counting than the first. It is an exercise to teach us to set a value on every day that God has given us to use. This is how we 'gain a heart of wisdom', without which we can never use time aright.

Numbering our days is to develop in us a right attitude to the time-span of life allotted to us. As Andrew Bonar expressed it:

Not many lives, but only one have we,
One — only one.
How sacred should that one life be!

Numbering our days is to impress on us *the brevity of life,* that from God's standpoint it is no more than 'a watch in the night' (Psalm 90:4). Time is important only because it prepares us for eternity. All the practical counsel that follows will not constrain us to redeem the time if the reality of eternity has never gripped us and the fear of God has never come upon us.

No motivation less than this is enough. For this we must seek God. Once we are motivated, here are the areas we must work on:

Find out what God wants

Before ever giving the exhortation to redeem the time, Paul says, 'Find out what pleases the Lord' (Ephesians 5:10). And immediately after giving it he adds, 'Understand what the Lord's will is' (v17).

The only person who succeeds in redeeming time is the one who fills it with doing God's will. But how can he do it unless he knows it? Since God is not a tyrant, the fact that he commands us to know his will must mean that this is possible for all of us.

The knowledge of God's will does not drop from heaven into the laps of passive believers. It has to be earnestly sought and prayed for, even as Paul sought it fervently for the Colossians (1:9). And no-one does that unless his heart attitude is one of submission, and his will is set to do the will of God.

Jesus put this very clearly when he said, 'If anyone chooses to do God's will, he will find out whether my teaching [which gives people direction] comes from God' (John 7:17). If we find it difficult or impossible to discern the will of God, the most likely cause is that our heart submission to the will of God is faulty.

If, however, your life is a perpetual rush and you never seem to have enough time to get everything done, it is very likely that you are packing your programme with numerous items that are surplus to the will of God.

Two facts should be self-evident. First, there is always time to do the will of God; and second, there is *not* time to do the will of God plus all the additional things that *you* want to do.

God's plan will certainly include time for rest, leisure and recreation, so that our depleted reserves of mental and physical energy may be restored. But it is all-too-easy in a pleasure-mad world for the Christian to get this aspect out of proportion. The love of sport and recreation or the pull of the TV screen can occupy too much time, and far more important things get crowded out.

Get your priorities right

Easier said than done. But if we are guilty of 'majoring on the minors and minoring on the majors', adjustments must be made — in the heart.

Do you find that you always have time for the things that you like doing even when there is no time for more important things? That means that self-will and self-pleasing rather than a passion for the will of God are determining your priorities. We often allow what we like best to 'jump the queue' and we lack the self-discipline to grab these 'gatecrashers' by the scruff of the neck and put them back in their place.

For the same reasons we consign the things we don't like doing to the back of the queue. The RSV has an interesting rendering of Ecclesiastes 8:3. Speaking of obeying the king's command, it says, 'Go from his presence, do not delay when the matter is unpleasant.'

Putting off an important task because it is difficult or unpleasant is a form of procrastination. There is grace available for the believer who knows he is weak in these areas to be self-disciplined in putting first things first. This is essential if we are to redeem the time.

Check your motivations

Behind much of our rush, impulsive action, taking on too much, striving and perpetual weariness is wrong motivation.

Do I take pride in 'my image'? Am I hounded by a fear of not making it? Is much of my drive really jealousy, competitiveness and rivalry? 'I saw that all labour and all achievement spring from man's envy of his neighbour' (Ecclesiastes 4:4). That is true of the world, but it should be no mark of the kingdom of God.

If some fail to redeem their time through wrong motivation, there are others who likewise fail through lack of motivation. 'We do not want you to become lazy, but to imitate those who through faith and patience inherit what has been promised' (Hebrews 6:12). Spiritual laziness is generally the result of lack of motivation.

Spiritual motives are sometimes mixed with carnal ambition and fleshly zeal. This leads to an unrealistic assessment of what we can accomplish in a given period of time. We start projects with a great burst of enthusiasm and much talk of what we are going to accomplish, 'by God's grace', of course, but there is not the time nor the will to see it through. So our drawers are full of incomplete schemes and studies.

But if my motives are pure and strong, I shall succeed in redeeming the time so that my life-work will not look like an unfinished symphony.

Watch those minutes

'Take care of the pennies and the pounds will take care of themselves.' The same principle applies to time. It is the small units we have to watch, not the big ones. Not many of us are guilty of wasting days, but what about the wasted minutes? Here is the leakage.

'Few men,' wrote Oswald Sanders, 'packed more into a lifetime than Dr F.B. Meyer. Of him it was said that he, like John Wesley, divided his life into spaces of five minutes, and endeavoured to make each one count for God.' According to his biographer, 'His calm manner was not the sleep of an inactive mind, it was more like the sleep of a spinning-top.'

'Wherever has the time gone? I seem to have done nothing.'

How often we have heard those words uttered, if we have not uttered them ourselves.

In the missionary training college my wife attended, new students were required to submit each week a full report on how each minute of the day had been spent, to impress upon them the sacredness of time, and how important it was to redeem it for God. This would be a valuable exercise for any Christian who is careless in his use of time. It would be an aid to self-discipline, until redeeming the minutes became as natural as breathing.

Snatch it from Satan

Paul tells us to redeem the time *'because the days are evil'*. Elsewhere he describes Satan as 'the god of this age' or time-span (2 Corinthians 4:4). In that kingdom where he rules, time is his tool, and through men and women he uses it for his evil ends. That is why the days are evil.

If we waste or misuse time, spend it for self and not for God, we are surrendering our 'pound' to the devil. Directly or indirectly, all unredeemed time is serving the devil's interests, if only because it is not serving the kingdom of God.

But the person who is determined to deny Satan as much as a minute of his time, and instead spend it for God, is effectively snatching time from the grasp of Satan and using it for his ultimate overthrow. Will you become a time-redeemer in the kingdom of God?

Called

A young man, hands in pockets, saunters aimlessly along a city street. Suddenly he feels a powerful grip on his shoulder. He turns to face the steely gaze of a police officer.

'Come with me,' he says. 'I have a warrant for your arrest.'

No longer is that young man free to wander the streets or frequent the pubs and clubs. He has been *apprehended.*

While the Almighty does not act like a policeman, he does apprehend people. Every child of God needs to know 'the agonising grip of God's hand' on his life. He needs to hear that compelling voice, 'Come with me,' and to recognise that he is no longer a free agent.

It was Paul's consuming desire to apprehend that purpose for which Christ had apprehended him. This is where the call of God begins.

Some, like Simon and Andrew, find Christ, and then subsequently receive a call to serve. Others, like Paul, receive it at the time of conversion. And I have met some who sensed even before they knew God that they were destined one day to serve him.

Few experience a call as dramatic as that of Abraham in Ur of the Chaldees, of Moses at the burning bush, or of Paul on the Damascus road. With most it comes slowly rather than suddenly, a growing conviction rather than a dramatic revelation, but it is none the less just as real and effectual.

The calling of God is not confined to the favoured few, those in full-time service, for example, or those with some outstanding gift or special ministry. 'Called, chosen and faithful' should be written across the life of every believer. But we can never expect to earn that commendation unless we *know* our calling.

The call of God not only gives us a sense of being apprehended by him, but also a sense of being *directed* in his path. The call of God has to do with our work in the kingdom, our function in the body of Christ.

Unlike the policeman, God does not apprehend us to lock us

up but to release us into a new and glorious path of spiritual activity. We are 'called according to his purpose', as Paul put it. He could speak from experience. At the time of his conversion the Lord told him through Ananias that he was a chosen vessel to bear his name before the Gentiles.

There is something wrong when believers of some years' standing are still asking, 'What is my ministry?' God wants them to know their calling.

Last but not least, to know our calling provides us with *motivation.* The service of God is not without its difficulties and discouragements, its setbacks and its sufferings. When the going is tough, when we cannot see the fruit of our labours, when we are tempted to 'chuck it in', what strength and determination it gives us to recall 'the ordination of the pierced hands'.

The discipline of resolve

'To make resolutions concerning our Christian lives, whether New Year ones or otherwise, is not only unnecessary, but tends to bring us into bondage. Under grace we are freed from striving to reach certain spiritual goals or standards. Just walk by faith. Let that new life within express itself. This is the way to grow into maturity. Straining for goals is not spiritual but carnal.'

This is the thinking of many who rightly feel the need to emphasise 'the grace in which we stand'. It is true that much teaching that has purported to be biblical has in fact been legalistic. Much striving for spirituality has been 'in the flesh', leading inevitably to failure and frustration. Nevertheless, we need to ask:

Are resolutions wrong?

Is it unnecessary to set ourselves spiritual goals? Is all resolving and striving fleshly? It is wonderfully true that under grace there is a spontaneous expression of the life of Christ in and through us. But is that the whole story?

Not only has God's Word something to say to us about this, but also the present experience of some who once came into wonderful release through the message of grace. When we find our progress grinding to a halt we have to ask ourselves, 'Is there something we have missed?'

When we come to think about it, purposing or resolving is something we are doing all the time, often unconsciously. It is the means by which we get things done. As humans we need this kind of incentive. Why should the spiritual life be any exception?

A church without spiritual goals will soon fossilise. If corporate goals are needful for the church, why not personal goals for the believer? David's resolve was to live a life of unbroken fellowship with God. Listen to this: 'One thing have I asked of the Lord, that will I seek after; that I may dwell in the house of the Lord all the days of my life' (Psalm 27:4 RSV).

Paul was possessed of a similar dedication of purpose: 'One thing I do, forgetting what lies behind and straining forward to what lies ahead, I press on toward the goal for the prize' (Philippians 3:13 RSV).

Singleness of purpose and the discipline of resolve have been vital ingredients in every story of spiritual success. Others, content to carry on without them, have spent their days in the shallows of spiritual mediocrity. Aim at nothing and you're sure to hit it!

Willing and doing

We must all agree that to have a right resolve is one thing; to fulfil it is something very different. Scripture recognises that with every resolution there is the willing and the doing. Paul makes mention of this in describing his battle with 'the flesh': 'I have the desire to do what is good,' he confesses, 'but I cannot carry it out' (Romans 7:18).

The Corinthian church had purposed to send a gift of money to their poorer brothers and sisters, but had been tardy in fulfilling this. So Paul exhorts them: 'Now therefore *perform* the doing of it; that as there was a readiness to will [a year ago], so there may be a performance' (2 Corinthians 8:11 KJV).

The failure of the man of the world to achieve any permanent success in fulfilling his good resolves is aptly illustrated by the words of Mark Twain: 'Giving up smoking is easy. I've done it lots of times!' But committed Christians, too, have a history of failure when it comes to performing their good intentions, and for basically the same reason.

What is that reason? It is that the individual, having made a decision of the will, relies on the *power* of the will to perform it. He then discovers, as Paul did in the statement already quoted (Romans 7:18), that *will-power* is in fact *will-weakness*. We are dealing with 'the will of the flesh', and the flesh is notoriously weak. Scripture hasn't one good word to say about it. It profits nothing, and even when it does succeed in performing, the result is 'dead works'.

If we would learn the open secret of achieving spiritual goals, our willing as well as our doing must come under the microscope. If our willing is not in God, then any prospect of our doing what we have willed is doomed before we start.

I may read the life of George Whitefield and be deeply challenged by the fact that he rose at five o'clock every morning and spent two or three hours praying and reading the Bible on his knees. This, his biographer tells me, was the secret of his spiritual success. I therefore resolve that I will from now on rise at 5.00 am for spiritual devotions.

Is this not a high and holy aspiration? It may be high without being holy! What are my motives for wanting to imitate the great preacher? Besides, there are numerous other practical factors that might well make what was fully in the will of God for Whitefield to be fully out of the will of God for me. The vital question is whether my resolve is born of God.

How to will aright

It has been asserted by some that Paul's last journey to Jerusalem, which led to his imprisonment, was not in the will of God. That he had taken the bit between his teeth and pressed ahead with his plan without heeding the warnings of what lay ahead, given him in the Spirit.

Personally, I feel instinctively cautious about theories of apostolic 'mistakes' that are not clearly and plainly recorded as such in Scripture. Here the question is, 'Was Paul's resolve to go up to Jerusalem born of God?' If so, we can take it that any subsequent warnings given by the Spirit were only to forewarn him, or test his resolve.

Acts 19:21 does not leave the issue in doubt: 'Paul *resolved in the Spirit to* . . . go to Jerusalem, saying, "After I have been there, I must also see Rome" ' (RSV). What does that mean? Simply that his resolution was inspired by the Holy Spirit.

Resolutions in the Christian life may be good and right, even essential, but they must have their origin in God and not in us. God must be in the willing as well as the doing. That's why Paul tells us, 'Work out your salvation with fear and trembling, for it is God who works in you to will and to act according to his good pleasure' (Philippians 2:12-13). I need to let God work in my will if I am to will rightly. And he will do it without robbing me of the free will he has given me.

This word to the Philippians provides the perfect balance between God's part and ours in this great business of doing 'his good pleasure'. It is not just the spontaneous expression of his life within. If the outworking was automatic, why the command, 'Work out . . .'?

No. Working the thing through so that the will of God is fulfilled requires me to do my part. God is working, but I am working, too. There must be on my part diligence and discipline, application and dedication. This is my response to what God is doing in me, and therefore is not in the flesh but in the Spirit.

The incentive is vital

Take this matter of rising each morning, a resolve we have to make every day. I know from statistics that most people do not die in road, rail or air accidents, but in their beds. Therefore I ought to get out of mine as swiftly as possible each morning!

Somehow, though, I never found this incentive ever got me out of bed on a cold morning. Many good resolves founder because the incentive is inadequate. One way God works in us to will his good pleasure is by creating powerful incentives in our thinking.

Paul does not simply tell the Philippians to work out their own salvation, but to do it *'with fear and trembling'*. Now that presupposes a powerful incentive. What was it? It is *the fact of God* — not God high in his heaven, but God within our very being. Not God present in a passive sense, but God, mighty and majestic, working powerfully in us to accomplish the goal on which we have set our hearts. Let that fact grip me and I have an incentive adequate for the fulfilling of my resolve.

Paul had just reminded them that they had always obeyed when he was present — and what believer wouldn't with that man of God around? But how much more should they obey now that he is absent. 'You may no longer be under my eagle eye, but you're under God's. I'm no longer working *among* you, but God is working in you. Realise that and your knees will knock.'

This fear of the Lord will solve many of our problems in the practical outworking of our salvation. It is this sense of the presence of God, and the true and rightful fear that it brings, that is one of the greatest needs in the present movement of the Holy Spirit.

The art of doing

If the ability to *will* comes from God, so does the power to *do*. Having worked in us to will, he does not then leave us to get on with it, but inspires the outworking of it. But it is not God apart from us, it is God in us, with us and through us.

Paul describes this perfectly, and from his own experience, when he says, 'For this I toil,' referring to his resolve to present every man mature in Christ, 'striving with all the energy which he mightily inspires within me' (Colossians 1:29 RSV).

What! Paul, the great apostle of grace, actually 'striving'? How unspiritual! Not when it is a striving inspired by the mighty working of God. But note that his goal, his resolve — the maturing of each saint — was from God. How ready God was to put forth his mighty power to accomplish that.

Then why is it, given a goal that is from God, we sometimes don't experience this mighty working of God? Simply lack of faith.

Paul states categorically, 'God is at work in you . . . to work for his good pleasure.' Do I believe it, count on it, right there in the dust and din of my spiritual workshop? If I do, his power is mightily released to do the job. If I don't, his power is limited, or even quenched.

Because I know that God is working in me, my work becomes 'a work of faith'. This is exactly what Paul prayed for the saints, 'that our God may . . . fulfil *every good resolve and work of faith by his power'* (2 Thessalonians 1:11 RSV).

As we press forward may it be with the full assurance that God will write across our worksheet at the end of the day, 'Target reached! Goal achieved!'

Don't be superspiritual

Superspirituality. It's so like the real thing. Most of us fall for it. Few of us recognise it. But all of us may be freed from it.

True spirituality is a thing of beauty and balance. It is winsome and attractive. It draws the outsider — and the insider. It is not self-conscious but the spontaneous expression of the Christ-life within. It is the work of the Holy Spirit. It springs from humility and the fear of God, from faith and love working in the heart.

But like most valuable things there is an imitation product which may all-too-easily pass for the real thing. The first thing is to be able to spot it.

What does it mean to be superspiritual? 'Super' is not used here to signify excellence, as when we exclaim, 'What a super day!' Taking the root meaning of the word as 'over' or 'beyond', it may signify 'in excess of what ought to be'. To be superspiritual, then, is to be *over*-spiritual, to go *beyond* the spirituality that God requires.

Because spirituality is a thing of balance, when we lose it we go overboard in one direction or another. This takes us into the realm of unreality, or even hypocrisy. Some prefer to call it *pseudo*-spirituality, that which has the semblance of the true, but is really false.

Let's look at some of the symptoms of this spiritual malaise, and also their root cause. Whether it be the gross form of the complaint displayed by the scribes and Pharisees, or the subtle, refined form that may appear even in the lives of dedicated believers, in essence it is the same.

Piety on parade

One of the first things Jesus denounced in these religious leaders was their wrong motivation. 'They do all their deeds to be seen by men' (Matthew 23:5 RSV). They were looking in the wrong direction — not upward for God's approval, but outward for people's approval. The places of honour at the feasts, the best seats in the synagogues, greetings in the market-places and being called 'Rabbi' — these were the things they were after.

Much earlier, when he was teaching his disciples the principles of the kingdom, Jesus warned them of the danger of performing their religious exercises — giving, praying or fasting — for the praise of men. If that was the reward they looked for, then that would be the only reward they would get (Matthew 6:2, 5, 16).

The fact that they were now his disciples did not mean that they were thereby free from the temptation which had floored their religious leaders. Wherever there is praying, preaching, exercising a spiritual gift or performing any other service for God, there is always the danger that men and women will parade their piety and thus divest it of true spirituality. 'Spiritual' activity minus a pure motive equals superspirituality, and that is obnoxious to God.

No-one is exempt

Jesus was rebuking the religionists of his day for being so concerned with the outside (appearances) at the expense of the inside (heart condition). This is called 'externalism' and it is a danger to which true believers, even charismatic ones, are continually prone.

While serving with the British forces in Egypt during the last war, I attended meetings that some missionaries had arranged for the troops. In one of the prayer meetings a young soldier was 'groaning in the Spirit'. I had never come across anything Pentecostal before, but having read books like *Praying Hyde,* I was suitably impressed.

My admiration evaporated later that evening, however, when the young man came forward at the close of a very simple gospel message to 'give his heart to Christ'. Whether this was a first time commitment, or whether he had been taught, 'You must be born again and again,' I wasn't sure. But I saw that the 'deep prayer life' was a bit of superspirituality that he had picked up from other Christians.

An earnest young man came to me the other day to talk about his desire to serve God. Two or three times in our brief conversation, when I said something that impressed him, he closed his eyes, drew in his breath sharply, and shuddered. You might think he needed deliverance. He did — from superspirituality!

The habit of bellowing out prayers and prophecies — presumably the full volume is designed to convince the hearers that the speaker is under a powerful anointing — the oohs and ahs, the stock phrases and exclamations that have become a mere form of words: all of these are no different in principle from the externalism that our Lord condemned in the scribes and Pharisees. The fact that they come from the lips of people who have received the Holy Spirit does not make them any the more acceptable to God.

When the root is right

By way of contrast, how beautiful are the expressions, loud or otherwise, that come from a heart moved by the Spirit.

Sometimes the murmur of praise may spread across a congregation, as gentle as the wind in the treetops. At other times it may be like 'a great multitude, like the roar of rushing waters and like loud peals of thunder' (Revelation 19:6).

Heaven, according to the apostle John, seems to be a rather noisy place. Half an hour's silence was so unusual it got a mention in the record! But heaven's noise is inspired by the Spirit. And that is what God wants on earth. When it happens, people whose hearts are open to God are not repelled. They sense God's presence. They are drawn in. They want to be involved.

But the desire to impress, to be well thought of, to receive commendation, even if we are hardly conscious of doing it, springs from one of the most subtle and devious forms of carnality — spiritual pride. The flesh knows how to 'talk humble' and 'act humble' while concealing the pride that lies deep within.

Sooner or later, however, it gives itself away, like the Christian who was so 'humble' that the church awarded him a medal. Then they had to take it from him because he wore it! Or the man who remarked that he wasn't a bit conceited, though he had every reason to be!

We are not to ask God to humble us. God says, 'Do it yourself' (see 1 Peter 5:6). 'But if *you* don't do it, I will, and then you'll really wish that you had!' We do need, however, to ask God to show us the roots of pride for what they are, and to enable us to extract them. Then we may begin to clothe ourselves with the beautiful garment of Christ's humility.

The factory or the garden?

True spirituality is 'the fruit of the Spirit', but the numerous forms of superspirituality are 'the works of the flesh' (Galatians 5:19-23 RSV). They are as different as the factory with its dust and din is different from the garden with its rest and relaxation.

Both the factory and the garden are productive, but the

method, and therefore the end-product, are radically different. The 'works' of the factory have their source in man, the creature. The 'fruit' of the garden has its source in God, the Creator. Some of us strive to produce the spirituality we see in others. But it is a striving of the flesh. It can only produce works, not fruit.

Striving has a tendency to generate tension, not only in ourselves, but in others, too. People find it hard to relax in our presence. We can be so activity-oriented that we drain those who are with us. After spending time with us they feel as though they have spent a day on the factory shopfloor. They want to escape to the garden.

Works! Works! Works! — and it's all so 'spiritual', but where is the fruit to satisfy the heart of the great Gardener?

Paul spoke of Jews going about to establish their own righteousness, and failing completely to achieve this because they did it apart from faith (Romans 10:3-4). Paul knew. Had he not been there himself?

We may be going about trying to establish our own spirituality. What do we produce? Superspirituality. Dead works. What is the missing ingredient? What is the root that produces the fruit?

Faith! God wants us to cease from our own works and enter into the rest of faith. 'Lord, I can't produce it, and I'm not going to try. But I do trust you to produce it in me.'

Off balance

Superspirituality is marked by imbalance. Like a caricature, it is out of proportion when you place it alongside the portrait of true spirituality.

Look at the scribes and Pharisees again. They were not content to tithe the income from the family business, but they tithed the produce from the patch of herbs they grew in their back garden. Nothing wrong with that except that they did it at the expense of basic kingdom principles. 'You tithe mint and dill and cummin, and have neglected the weightier matters of the law, justice and mercy and faith . . . . You blind guides, straining out a gnat and swallowing a camel!' (Matthew 23:23-24 RSV). False spirituality has a tendency to major on minors and minor on majors.

Scripture teaches that commitment to a local body of believers involves commitment to assemble with them. But this is the sort of area in which false spirituality may go overboard. One recalls the Christian woman married to an unconverted husband. Her zeal for attending meetings meant that often her husband had to get his own meal when he came back late from work, and then put the children to bed.

In another, less extreme, case the wife had to be counselled to cease attending every meeting and start putting some of her spiritual zeal into the fulfilment of her marital and maternal responsibilities. Before we add our 'Tut, tut!' let's check out whether in other areas we are not as guilty.

Going beyond the word

It began in the garden of Eden. 'Did God say, "You shall not eat of any tree?"' asked the serpent. He knew quite well that was not what God had said. It was only one tree that was forbidden. His aim was to discredit God in the woman's thinking.

She corrected this error only to make a similar error herself: 'God said, "You shall not eat of the fruit of the tree which is in the midst of the garden, *neither shall you touch it,* lest you die."'

Whenever had God said that *touching* the fruit would result in death? It was going beyond the word of God.

The Pharisees were the die-hard fundamentalists of Judaism. They would never take away anything of the Scriptures or deny the concept of resurrection, as the Sadducean liberals did. They simply added to them until they were so encrusted with their own traditions that no-one could distinguish between the two. In this way they bound 'heavy burdens, hard to bear . . . on men's shoulders'.

Fundamental evangelicalism has always been a fruitful field for this kind of superspirituality. They would never say that 1 Corinthians 12 or 14 is not inspired. They just add the little corollary, 'It's not for today,' and so make it of no effect.

In many areas of Christian behaviour, such as Sunday observance, cinema-going or touching alcohol, there are the unwritten rules, and adherence to them becomes a yardstick for measuring a person's spirituality. These things only serve to obscure the nature of the spirituality that God wants, which is a thing of heart attitude.

It would take a book to expose the innumerable manifestations of this hydra-headed monster. Superspirituality rears its ugly head in the most unexpected places. There is no better solution to the problem than a baptism of the fear of God, for behind so much of it is a false or inadequate concept of God.

'You have loved righteousness and hated lawlessness' was what the Father said of his Son. True spirituality involves loving and hating. The fear of God will cause us to feel about false spirituality as God feels about it — and he hates it. It will also put into our hearts his passion for the real.

It is not enough to abandon the factory. We must find our way into the garden. It is not enough to denounce the caricature. We must display the true likeness of Christ.

Baptism in the Holy Spirit

On the Goshen estate the blood that had been painted on the lintel and doorpost of each house was still wet. The smell of roast lamb pervaded every home.

Each family was in a state of suppressed excitement and of feverish activity. Household chattels had been tied in bundles, ready to be borne on head or shoulder. Every robe was belted at the waist and every foot sandalled in readiness for the coming march. Round the fire they crouched to eat their hasty meal — meat, unleavened bread and bitter herbs.

As the first grey streaks spread across the eastern sky, each Israelite father led his family out to join the great exodus. After four hundred years a nation was coming out of slavery into freedom. 'Redeemed!' they shouted to one another, as they turned their backs on Egypt for ever.

Baptism in cloud and sea

At the head of the long marching column they could see a pillar of cloud that was mysteriously unaffected by the morning breeze. It moved before them, never so slowly that the marchers had to dawdle or so quickly that the old or the young could not keep up.

At the Red Sea, Moses, their leader, parted the waters for the final phase of Israel's initiation into their new life as God's people. When all had crossed, the waters returned, not only destroying the pursuing Egyptians but also cutting Israel off for ever from their past life. Old things had passed away, and all things had become new.

This is one of the Bible's most graphic pictures of Christian initiation. 'Our forefathers were all under the cloud and . . . they all passed through the sea. They were all baptised into Moses in the cloud and in the sea . . . . These things . . . were written down as warnings for us' (1 Corinthians 10:1-2, 11).

What is the 'one baptism'?

'There is . . . one Lord, one faith, one baptism,' says Paul

(Ephesians 4:5). Does he mean baptism in water or baptism in the Spirit? He means *the 'one baptism' into Christ* which involves both water and Spirit.

This word about Israel's baptism into Moses beautifully illustrates this. They were 'under the cloud' that enveloped and led them, picturing baptism in the Spirit. They also 'passed through the sea', prefiguring water baptism. So Israel's redemption by blood was sealed by a twin baptism into Moses in cloud and sea. And this is 'for our instruction'. But what does it teach us?

God's people under the new covenant need to be initiated into Christ as his old covenant people were initiated into Moses, that is, by a baptism in cloud and sea. Neither water baptism nor Spirit baptism is an optional extra for the committed Christian.

If we profess Christ as our example then we must follow in his steps. Though he was the sinless Son he submitted to being immersed by John in the Jordan river. As he came up out of the water the heavens were opened and the Holy Spirit came upon him. This was 'when he began' (Luke 3:23 literally). This was his messianic initiation. He was also blazing a trail for us to follow.

First foundation class

At Pentecost Peter took his convicted hearers through the first foundation class in the history of the church. He told them to repent, be baptised and receive the Holy Spirit (Acts 2:38).

Tracing through the Acts record we find that water baptism and Spirit baptism are constantly linked. It was so with the converts in Samaria (8:14-17). It was so with Saul of Tarsus (9:17-18). It was so in the Gentile outpouring in Caesarea (10:47-48). And it was so in Ephesus (19:5-6).

In his epistles Paul never tells the young churches he had founded to get baptised or receive the Holy Spirit. He takes it for granted that they have been initiated, and appeals to them on that ground.

Paul could make that sort of assumption only because he and his fellow-workers had been personally involved in laying these foundations in the lives of their converts. What he would do today if confronted with the hotchpotch of Christendom is perhaps suggested by his handling of the twelve disciples he found in Ephesus, in whose spiritual beginnings he had played no part. Sensing a missing dimension in their spiritual experience, he asked, 'Did you receive the Holy Spirit when you believed?' (Acts 19:2).

At no point did Paul ask them about the reality of their faith, but inquired whether their believing had been accompanied by a reception of the Spirit. He soon discovered that they were John the Baptist's disciples. John could only take his disciples as far as he had gone himself. He truly believed in Jesus as the Messiah, but had never come into the full blessing of the new covenant.

Paul knew at once what these disciples needed, which is also needed by countless professing Christians in the churches today. It was the 'one baptism'. It was full initiation into Christ. So he first immersed them in water in the name of Christ, and then laid hands on them for the Holy Spirit. They all spoke in tongues and prophesied.

Did you receive?

Let me put that question to my readers: 'Did *you* receive the Holy Spirit when you believed?' Then let me anticipate some answers that I feel sure would be given.

Someone will reply: 'Of course I have received the Holy Spirit. You cannot belong to Christ without having the Spirit of Christ, can you? I know I belong to Christ, so I must have received the Spirit.'

It is true that Paul teaches that every believer has the Spirit of Christ. But I am sure that Paul would be decidedly unhappy with that kind of reasoning, for to him and to all the early Christians, receiving the Spirit was not theoretical, nor even merely theological, but experiential.

Having the Spirit does not preclude you from the need to *receive* the Spirit. Jesus surely had the Spirit for the first thirty years of his life on earth. But at the Jordan the Spirit came to him in a new and different way.

This is prefigured in the grain offering of Leviticus 2:5-6. Like all the offerings it speaks of Christ, and so of his body. It was to be of 'fine flour . . . without yeast' — our Lord's holy humanity. It was to be 'mixed with oil' — his union with the Holy Spirit. They were to 'break it in pieces' (RSV) — his utter self-surrender to death, as expressed in his baptism. Finally they were to 'pour oil on it' — his anointing with the Holy Spirit. The offering had to have oil *on* it as well as *in* it. How accurate are the Old Testament types!

What it means to receive

Returning to my question, some would reply by saying, 'I'm not sure what exactly you mean by "receiving the Holy Spirit."'

Tracing through its use in the Acts and the epistles proves that receiving the Spirit is not identical with receiving Christ. Conversion to Christ and the baptism in the Spirit are not the same, though we do have one solitary instance of both happening to individuals at the same time (Acts 10:44-48).

The word that is used consistently and repeatedly to describe what happens in the baptism in the Spirit, but is never used simply of conversion, is 'upon'. The Old Testament prepares us for this. Anointing oil was poured *upon* the head of prophet, priest and king, not to make them God's people, for they were that already, but to fit them for their special service. God put the Spirit that was *upon* Moses *upon* the elders of Israel to equip them for leadership (Numbers 11:25 RSV).

The Spirit coming *upon* the Lord Jesus at the Jordan was not to make him more holy than he was — an impossibility — but in order that the words and works of God, never before associated with the carpenter's son, might be manifested in him.

He in turn promised the disciples that they would be 'endued [clothed *upon*] with power from on high' when they received the Holy Spirit. So it was on the day of Pentecost. Later in the Acts we read how the Spirit came *upon,* fell *upon,* and was poured *upon* different groups of disciples. Paul reminds Titus of 'the Holy Spirit which he poured out *upon* us richly'. Have *you* had an 'upon' experience of the Holy Spirit?

How may we know?

Some would answer my question this way: 'There was an occasion some time after my conversion when I surrendered myself to God and asked him to fill me with his Spirit. It was a wonderful experience at the time. Since then there have been moments when I have felt the presence and power of the Holy Spirit in my life, but I've never been really sure that I have been baptised in the Spirit.'

God wants us to have an *enduring* experience. 'He on whom you see the Spirit *descend and remain,* this is he . . . .' This was how John the Baptist was to identify his Messiah (John 1:32-34 RSV).

'Descend and remain' was a key phrase. It tells us that the age of preparation was dying and the age of fulfilment was dawning. Under the old covenant the Spirit descended on men and women, but under the new he would descend and *remain.* This was the Comforter that Jesus promised 'to be with you for ever'. We are not to settle for an experience that comes and goes when we have been promised one that abides.

Jesus also wanted us to be quite sure that we have received. 'Wait for the promise of the Father,' he told his disciples. Implicit in those words was the assurance that they would know when the promise had been fulfilled. How else would they have known how long to wait? We are not to expect the confirmation of a rushing mighty wind or cloven tongues of fire, for that wasn't in the promise. How then are we to know?

What is the sign?

Is speaking in tongues the sign? Did Jesus say, 'You shall receive *tongues* when the Holy Spirit has come upon you'? No, he said, 'You shall receive *power* . . . .'

We must put the emphasis where Jesus put it. Power is the essential ingredient. Power to be, power to do, power to function according to our gift and calling in the body of Christ.

'Should we not expect to speak in tongues?' Yes. The Acts record confirms that this is the normal manifestation when the Spirit comes upon people. But we are not to seek for tongues as the be-all and end-all of the experience. This may all-too-easily result in a shallow if not spurious experience.

I have met a few believers who have received power without tongues. They simply need a release into the charismatic dimension. I have met all-too-many who seem to have tongues without power. Many of these need to be seeking God afresh for an enduement with power, which is what Christ promised. By and large you get what you seek.

How to receive

Though it is essential to be convinced of the scriptural basis of the experience, this alone is not enough. There must be a deep desire for God to meet us in this way. Jesus set out this basic condition when he said, 'If any man thirst let him come to me and drink.' Only the thirsty qualify.

If you are not thirsty, ask God to show you why. Often there is inner adjustment needed — cleansing from sin, righting wrong attitudes or motives, deliverance from fear or unbelief. Then we suddenly find that mental assent to a biblical proposition has turned into spiritual thirst.

Then you must come to the Lord in prayer, pleading the promises that God has quickened to you. Jesus said, 'Come to me and drink.' That means not only *asking* in faith, but *taking* in faith. This is the faith that appropriates the blessing, and says, 'Thank you.'

The ministry of laying on of hands by a mature, Spirit-filled believer may greatly help you here to shift gear from the place of asking to the place of taking, and then again into a manifestation in tongues. Remember God is for you. He is not looking for grounds to disqualify you but for a reason to bless you. 'How much more will your heavenly Father give the Holy Spirit to [you] who ask him.'

Finally, remember that the baptism in the Spirit is part of Christian initiation. That means a beginning, not an end. It is getting our feet on the foothills of the Spirit, not planting a flag on the top of Everest!

Some of us have been on the mountain for many years, and we find there is still so much to explore and experience. To those who have not yet tasted life in the Spirit, who may be hesitating to venture forth, we would say, 'Come on up. It's great!'

Develop your faith and move that mountain!

Do you have a fully developed faith?

You may have the faith of endurance, to wait patiently for a prayer to be answered or a promise to be fulfilled. Or you may have the faith of fortitude, to endure when all seems to have gone wrong, or when called to endure opposition or misunderstanding. And yet you may be short on that inspirational type of faith that can speak to situations and command them to change.

As well as persevering in prayer until we receive answers, God wants to develop in us an ability to prevail before the answer comes, and to start thanking God in anticipation of that answer. He not only wants us to resist the enemy's activity but to exercise authority in binding him and so neutralising his activity.

This sort of inspirational faith is vital for accomplishing the work of God's kingdom. It releases faith in others. It creates spiritual momentum when all seems to be static. Jesus was referring to this kind of faith when he spoke of its ability to move mountains (Matthew 17:20; 21:21) or to uproot trees and throw them into the sea (Luke 17:6).

Leaves or fruit?

It was when Jesus cursed the fig tree that he spoke for the second time about moving mountains. Lodging each night at Bethany, he journeyed into the city each morning to teach in the temple. This particular morning he was hungry, and approached a fig tree to see if it had any fruit. Finding nothing but leaves, he said to the tree, 'May no-one ever eat fruit from you again' (Mark 11:12-14).

A little comment here by Mark — 'it was not the season for figs' (v13) — has been a useful handle for those looking for a way to attack our Lord. 'He was acting out of pique,' they would tell us, 'cursing a fig tree for not satisfying his hunger when it was not the season for fruit.'

The fact is that Jesus had grounds for expecting fruit because the tree was in leaf. The fig tree produces edible green knobs known as 'taksh' when the leaves first appear in March, but the main crop comes in June. The absence of 'taksh' on a tree in leaf suggests that it was a barren tree.

The context of this incident — it was immediately before Jesus drove the hucksters and tricksters from the temple, rebuking them for turning his Father's house into a den of robbers — suggests that this miracle was also a parable. The fig tree pointed to Israel, about to come under the divine curse, not because of its barrenness, but because of its great religious pretensions without any spiritual reality. It had plenty of leaves but no fruit.

The Gentile nations, of course, were also barren, but they made no pretence of possessing true spirituality. Israel professed so much — the outward foliage of religion — but with no fruit to satisfy the hungry Saviour.

You will recall that Adam and Eve in the garden used fig leaves to hide their nakedness. Now Israel was using the foliage of empty forms and external observances to hide her spiritual barrenness.

But this is not only a parable for Israel, it is a parable for us — born-again, Spirit-baptised believers though we may be. We may sing the right songs, perform the right actions, talk the right jargon, subscribe to the right theology, go through the right motions, but is it foliage or fruit?

In his day, Paul referred to those who wanted 'to make a good impression outwardly' (Galatians 6:12), who had 'a form of godliness but denying its power' (2 Timothy 3:5). They are still with us.

No fruit means no reality. Fruit is not the product of religious activity; it is the product of the life of God working in us. Are we, like Israel, characterised by works instead of faith, leaves without fruit? That adds up to unreality.

'Land that drinks in the rain often falling on it [people enjoying the blessing of the Spirit] and that produces a crop . . . receives the blessing of God. But land that produces thorns and thistles [despite the rain that falls on it] is worthless and is in danger of being cursed. In the end it will be burned' (Hebrews 6:7-8).

We all need to make an honest assessment. We cannot afford to do less.

For the 'whosoever'

Whether or not the disciples saw at that time that the fig tree was a picture of their own nation is not clear. But when, the following morning, Peter drew our Lord's attention to the withered tree, Jesus immediately applied the lesson to them.

'Have faith in God,' he said. Israel, devoid of faith, was spiritually barren and concealed the fact with religious activity. 'I don't want you to be like that,' Jesus would seem to say. 'I want you to be characterised by faith.'

'I tell you the truth,' Jesus continued — and he needed a preface like that to the incredible statement that was to follow — 'if anyone says to this mountain, "Go, throw yourself into the sea," and does not doubt in his heart but believes that what he says will happen, it will be done for him' (Mark 11:23).

True, Jesus was addressing his apostles, but he does not confine the promise to them or to any other particular class of person in the church. There is no suggestion that you have to qualify as an elder or deacon, or in fact to be a leader at all.

In the old King James Version 'anyone' is 'whosoever'. This is the word that gave us hope when we first heard the good news and wondered if we qualified. 'The gospel of the whosoever,' we were told, 'includes *you*.'

But let this promise of Jesus now sink into our hearts. The exercise of dynamic, mountain-moving faith is open to the 'whosoever' — and that means you and me, whether leader or follower, man or woman, old or young in the faith, provided only that we will dare to include ourselves in it.

Why a mountain?

I love mountains. I have gazed in wonder at the Rockies of North America, and the Alps of Switzerland, at the mountains of Wales and the Scottish Highlands. I have no desire to see any of these thrown into the sea! Jesus is not encouraging us to move mountains for a pastime. What he is saying is that *there are 'mountains' that must be moved in the interests of the kingdom.*

Centuries before Jesus spoke these words, Isaiah had predicted a day of divine visitation when the glory of the Lord would be revealed, and all flesh would see it together. 'Every valley shall be raised up,' he declared, 'every mountain and hill made low' (Isaiah 40:3-5). In other words there would be a filling-in of the voids and a removal of the obstacles that hindered the movement of God.

We cannot but be aware of the 'mountains', the mighty ones and the mini-ones, that stand in the way of God's moving in our day. A 'mountain' may be purely satanic or it may be apparently human. It may be circumstantial or financial. If it is hindering the purpose of God it is a 'mountain' to be moved.

It waits to be challenged by the 'whosoever' who will dare to believe the promise of God.

Paul and Barnabas, on their first missionary journey, faced a 'mountain' in the island of Cyprus. It took the form of a Jewish sorcerer. He was an attendant of the Roman official of the place, a man who was showing keen interest in the gospel. The sorcerer openly opposed Paul, and tried to turn the proconsul from the faith. In Acts 13:9-12 we read how Paul cast that mountain into the sea. It brought the Roman official to true faith in Christ.

A Spirit-filled missionary I knew was preaching in the open air in a Muslim area of North India when one of his listeners was seized by an evil spirit. It was useless to continue preaching. Every eye was watching to see whether this 'Jesus' being preached could break the hold of Satan.

Addressing the evil spirit, the missionary commanded it to come out. There was no response.

'God, what do I do now?' was his desperate cry. 'Your name is at stake!'

'Proclaim the victory,' came the inner whisper.

Boldly the preacher declared how Christ was made flesh and overcame darkness, disease and death. How he broke Satan's hold at the cross, and rose again to prove that he'd done it. How he ascended on high far above all principality and power — 'And now, I command you, unclean spirit, to come out of him,' he cried. And out of him it came.

How do you get there?

'If anyone . . . does not doubt in his heart, but believes that what he says will happen, it will be done for him.' It sounds tremendous, but how do you get there?

'Such faith is beyond my grasp,' you may say. 'I'm afraid of being carried away with human enthusiasm, of using a false faith which is no more than presumption. I fear that I would speak the words only to fall flat on my face.'

Let me remind you again that Jesus' words, 'If anyone says . . . it will be done for him,' are not to tease you or lead you up the garden path but to impress on you that *you are included in this promise.* Jesus is saying, '*You* can do it!'

Begin to respond to God. Tell him what he's telling you. 'Lord, this promise is for me, even me. I can move mountains!' Your very confession will do something for you.

Jesus followed the promise with this important statement: 'Therefore I tell you, whatever you ask for in prayer, believe that you have received it, and it will be yours' (Mark 11:24).

Strictly speaking, talking to mountains is not prayer. When you pray you talk to God, not to mountains. But Jesus' postscript was about prayer as the key to the kind of faith that he was talking about. We must learn how to talk to God before we can talk to the mountain.

One could call this the great 'praying through' verse of the Bible. 'Believe that you *have* received it' — past tense, 'and it *will* be yours' — future tense.

Do not assume that a day will dawn when suddenly and mysteriously you will find an inspiration of faith that can command mountains into the sea of oblivion. People working on this false assumption are still waiting for it to work.

Jesus gives us the key. 'Whatever you ask for in prayer, believe that you have received it.' Again, this faith of which Jesus is speaking is not something we can switch on. We find it because we seek it in prayer. The crisis of commanding the mountain is the result of a process of faith that is effected through prayer.

Encircle before you command

Do you remember how Jericho was conquered? The city had come under siege and God had said to Joshua, 'See, I have delivered Jericho into your hands' (Joshua 6:2). Then Joshua and the people were told to march around the city once a day for six days. On the seventh day they were to march around seven times and then give a loud shout. They did this and the walls fell down flat.

The significance of that shout of faith was that it was commanding this physical obstacle, the walls, to be removed. But notice, it didn't happen the first day. First there had to be the encompassing of the city day after day. There was a rising of faith with each circuit. Circling the city seven times on the seventh day speaks of faith reaching the point of fulfilment. The shout of faith was simply the culmination of the process.

Do not suppose that 'mountains', as Jesus spoke of them, are always dramatically satanic, like the case of Elymas, the sorcerer who confronted Paul in Cyprus, or the man seized with a demon in North India. They may simply be circumstances that are being used by Satan to hinder God's work. They still call for the exercise of authority and faith to order them into the sea.

Not long ago I was praying for my brother, Peter, who had moved at God's direction from Sussex to Devon but had not succeeded in selling his house, although it had been on the market for a long time. He was therefore unable to purchase a house in Devon, and was living there with relatives. At the same time he had procured another car, and every effort to sell the old one was equally unsuccessful. All this was not only financially embarrassing but hindering him in the starting up of a new business.

As I prayed I became increasingly convinced that this was a situation that God did not want us to tolerate any longer. Here, surely, was a mountain waiting to be moved, and I started to take it regularly in prayer to God. After a few days I found myself one morning telling the mountain to go. There were no dramatics. I just spoke the word once and noted it in my diary.

Now I was no longer praying over the situation, having assurance that God had heard, but daily waiting for a letter or telephone call with news of a breakthrough. However, no news came. Had I got my wires crossed? Had I acted presumptuously?

Two weeks later I met my brother in Devon and enquired about the situation. 'Oh, haven't you heard?' he said. 'The house in Sussex sold and we have had our offer accepted for a house here, which we are delighted with. Oh, and I managed to sell the car about the same time.'

'But you never told me,' I complained.

'Well, it all happened so suddenly — about two weeks ago!'

Most of us don't need to search for the 'mountains' that impede the progress of the kingdom — they are all around us. Accommodation not available, a 'chain' holding up the buying and selling of a house, the locking up of finances or the blocking of authorisation from some local authority.

Then there are spiritual blockages in human lives, hindering people from finding Christ or coming into spiritual fulness and release. Others are earnestly desiring yet failing to find their spiritual setting so that they may bloom where God has planted them.

Whether these personally apply to us or refer to situations with which we are acquainted, they constitute a call to the 'whosoever' to prove the promise of Jesus: *'If anyone says to this mountain, "Go, throw yourself into the sea" . . . it will be done for him.'*

Wanted: Men of violence

We live in a world full of violence.

Recently there was a massive police hunt for a man who abducted a three-year-old girl, sexually assaulted her and then threw her, bound and gagged, into the canal, where she drowned. Since then there has been a spate of child abductions and tragic deaths.

We have seen violence on our football terraces, violence in Northern Ireland, violence in South Africa. We are sick and tired of violence.

It is therefore something of a shock when we are informed by none other than our Lord and Master that the taking of his kingdom — whatever that means — calls for violent men.

Predicting end-time events, Jesus said that kingdom would rise against kingdom (Matthew 24:7). That means war. The appearance of the kingdom of God inevitably resulted in a clash of spiritual kingdoms — in other words, spiritual warfare.

Warfare, as we all know, is never gentle. It is the most universal and unrestrained form of violence in the world. Jesus spoke of his kingdom in terms of an invasion designed to drive out Satan from the territory he had illegally occupied (Matthew 12:28). Satan never voluntarily relinquishes his grasp on the territory he holds; he has to be forced to do so, and that involves violence.

Once we acknowledge the fact that there is *spiritual* as well as *physical* warfare, it becomes clear that there must be spiritual as well as physical violence. This, said Jesus, is how the kingdom will be taken.

Taking the kingdom

Taking the kingdom was predicted back in the Old Testament: 'The saints of the Most High shall *take* the kingdom, and possess the kingdom for ever, even for ever and ever' (Daniel 7:18 KJV).

It is a pity that later versions have 'receive' or 'possess' the kingdom instead of 'take' the kingdom. Although this is equally accurate, it is a passive concept. 'Take' is active and dynamic. To 'take' and 'possess' a kingdom suggests warfare (see also Psalm 149:6-9), and this is what Jesus is teaching when he says: 'The kingdom of heaven suffers violence, and violent men take it by force' (Matthew 11:12 NASB).

What then is involved in the taking of the kingdom? It helps when we understand that the kingdom of God is the *rule* of God. To take the kingdom means to *dispossess* Satan of the territory which he has wrongfully taken and to establish in its place the rule of heaven.

When a person turns his life over to Christ, and submits to him as Lord, the kingdom (or rule) has come within him. When a father and mother bring their family under the rule of Christ by applying in the home the principles of the kingdom — there the kingdom has come. When a businessman does the same with his business, he is extending the kingdom through his business.

So the taking of the kingdom, or the coming of the kingdom, does not await the return of Jesus, although that will be the moment when the takeover is completed (Revelation 11:15). Daniel teaches us that it is the saints of the Most High — that is, believers — who take the kingdom, while Jesus says it is the violent ('men' does not occur in the Greek) who take it by force.

Putting the two passages together we learn that the saints, both men and women, are to take the kingdom by violence.

The current attitude

The IRA terrorists are men of violence. To them the bomb and the bullet are perfectly legitimate ways of accomplishing their 'kingdom' goal — a united Ireland.

They have no normal home life. They are pursued and harried by the authorities. They could be arrested and locked up at any time. Occasionally they are the victims of their own bombs, or die by an opponent's bullet. But they consider all that to be an acceptable sacrifice for the great cause. You have to hand it to them — they are totally dedicated. Violent men who fight for a cause always are.

When we switch to the spiritual, how does the goal of a united Ireland compare with the kingdom of this world becoming the kingdom of our God and of his Christ? Or the Son of God and Lord of Glory seeing of the travail of his soul, after two thousand years, and being satisfied (Isaiah 53:11 RAV)? Or the earth being filled with the glory of God as the waters cover the sea (Habakkuk 2:14)?

Does not the goal of the Irish terrorist pale into insignificance by comparison? Where, then, are the men and women of comparable dedication who will fulfil that for which Christ has been waiting so long: to see his enemies made his footstool (Psalm 110:1)? Where are the Pauls who will say: 'I am ready not only to be bound, but also to die in Jerusalem for the name of the Lord Jesus' (Acts 21:13)?

Laid back

Rather than anything comparable, we seem to find in Christian circles — even the most enlightened ones — a striking contrast.

We want to have our Christianity easy and comfortable. It must not make too heavy a demand on our private lives. Everything must be jolly and joyful. Don't ever mention the words 'sacrifice' or 'self-discipline'. Modern life is so full, there is so much on, that leaders should not expect too much spiritually of the saints.

To be white hot for God is no longer in vogue. The feeling abroad is that we must be relaxed and 'laid back' in our spirituality.

'Don't get carried away in your zeal for the kingdom — it's out of fashion!' seems to be the attitude.

'People who are over-enthusiastic,' we are warned, 'are usually superspiritual, and that means a forced spirituality. We must have the real thing!'

'Beware of extremism and fanaticism,' say other people. 'You'll turn worldly people off!'

Look at the way we pray. This is where the battle for the kingdom is meant to be fought. But you wouldn't think so by our casual approach. In the first place, if it's nothing more than a meeting for prayer, we attend only if we don't have anything more important on.

Listening to the prayers, one would never imagine that we were engaged in spiritual warfare. Often we display a familiarity with the Almighty — 'God and I are good buddies' — that seems to be devoid of that quality of *awe* that is appropriate to his majestic nature. There *is* a familiarity that God delights in, but it is shot through with a fear of God, and that is a quality that seems to be in short supply.

If we have got caught up in this spirit, we need to look again at the life of Jesus. He was both an *extremist* and a *fanatic*. When the disciples saw him in burning anger drive out the moneychangers from the temple, they remembered that it was written: 'Zeal for your house will consume me' (John 2:17).

Let us then consider the nature of these violent men whom Christ said are taking the kingdom. They are marked by:

1. The violence of self-discipline

Violent men are always intolerant of what they see as thwarting their purpose. It must be exterminated. In our case we are not called to wage war against the *speck of dust* in our brother's eye, but to battle against the *plank of wood* in our own (Luke 6:41-42).

There is an inner war that we have first to win. It involves the sinful desires and character weaknesses that Peter tells us 'war against your soul' (1 Peter 2:11). The answer to this is the cross, which is a violent way of putting someone to death (see Galatians 5:24).

In addition to fighting the positively sinful, there is the whole area of keeping our bodies under control so that they are our servants and not our masters.

The love of ease and the continual desire to give in to natural desires is universal. The great Augustine used to pray that he might have 'toward God a heart of flame, toward men a heart of love, and toward himself a heart of steel'. Paul took the same attitude. He said, 'I beat my body' — that's fairly violent! — 'and make it my slave so that after I have preached to others, I myself will not be disqualified for the prize' (1 Corinthians 9:27).

Servants of God need to recognise that failure to exercise this form of violence could rob them of their reward at the judgment seat of Christ.

2. The violence of intercession

Prayer warfare is a violent attack on the kingdom of darkness. Paul reminds us that our struggle 'is not against flesh and blood' but against the spirit forces in the heavenly realms (Ephesians 6:12).

The prayer effort to take the kingdom is sometimes portrayed in terms of warfare. At other times it is described as a wrestling contest (Colossians 4:12) or the binding of an opponent before plundering his house (Matthew 12:29).

Fasting is a God-appointed means by which we may strengthen the force of intercession, bind the adversary and render him powerless, or force him to quit (see Isaiah 58:6).

The praying that precedes revival is more often than not this violent type. There is an urgency and an importunity about it that *refuses to take no for an answer.* It is like the prayer of Jacob at Peniel when he cried out: 'I will not let you go unless you bless me' (Genesis 32:26).

James Burns, speaking of the period preceding a widespread awakening, describes the sense of deep dissatisfaction, weariness and aching void that fills the hearts of God's people: 'Slowly this aching grows, the heart of man begins to cry out for God, for spiritual certainties, for fresh visions. From a faint desire this multiplies as it widens, until it becomes a vast human need; until in its urgency it seems to *beat with violence* at the very gates of heaven.'

The kind of praying we so often experience is far removed from this holy importunity of the Spirit. How we need God to pour out upon us the spirit of grace and supplication!

3. The violence of dynamic faith

Violent faith springs out of, and cannot be separated from, the violence of intercession. Faith is spiritual dynamite. Jesus spoke a word of faith to the fig tree and caused it to wither from the roots. In the same context he taught his disciples that, if they had faith, they could move mountains (Mark 11:12-24).

The man of faith is a *violent* man. He can release spiritual forces. He can part the waters of the Red Sea. He can throw down the walls of Jericho. He can put the armies of Satan to flight.

This faith that we all covet cannot be obtained apart from the other two qualities. It flows out of self-discipline and prayer. 'There is nothing which lies beyond the power of prayer save that which lies outside of the will of God.'

God is looking for men and women of *holy violence.* Let us get into training. Let us sharpen and use the weapon of prayer. May we be registered in heaven as those violent saints who *take the kingdom.*

Relationships — time for a check-up

There are more exciting themes than relationships, but none more important. We may prefer to read about 'the present triumph of the kingdom', but that will never be more than a pipe-dream if we don't get our relationships right.

Many of us are activists. We are keen to see our ministry develop, to reach our full potential in God, to move in faith. All highly commendable. But from time to time God has to bring us up with a jolt to make us realise that what we *are* is more important than what we *do.* And the most tell-tale indication of what we are is the state of our relationships.

Relationships will radically affect our doing, but really they have more to do with being than doing. A breakdown in relating is a character failure rather than a ministry failure.

Loners may sometimes have a highly developed and seemingly successful ministry, but in some vital area of character they are deficient. God designed man to be a sociable creature, so that the loner is acting out of character. Certainly his ministry would be more effective if he overcame his inbred reluctance to relate to others.

'The church is not buildings but people' — so runs the well-worn evangelical cliche. But God is now teaching us that the church is not simply people, but *people in relationship*.

The figure for the church that Paul loved most, and that he alone used, was a many-membered body. Our physical bodies are the means by which we express ourselves, and they perform many functions to do this.

There was a time when we got so excited because God was giving us a vision of the kind of church he wanted, functioning in the power of the Spirit and moving with divine authority, just as we see it doing in the Acts of the Apostles. But then God had to take us further back and show us that there will never be proper function without proper relationship.

The church is not a vast conglomeration of unrelated parts. As a *building* it is composed of living stones, but a pile of stones on a site doesn't make a building. It is only as the stones and other materials are brought into a certain relationship by the skill of the builder that a building is formed.

It may be a gruesome thought, but with the progress of 'spare part surgery' it is conceivable that one day there may be hospital 'banks' with every kind of physical organ, all ready for emergency use. But no such collection would be a body. The church is the body of Christ because it has been baptised in the Holy Spirit into one organic whole (1 Corinthians 12:13).

A broken ankle radically affects the relationship of the foot with the rest of the body. So you have a complete person on crutches because the foot cannot function. I believe we would all be horrified if God were to show us the measure in which the body of Christ is needlessly incapacitated and its full potential never realised because of 'broken ankles', 'sprained wrists', 'dislocated shoulders' and many other disjointed parts.

Don't say that you are too busy getting on with the job to concern yourself with something so intangible as relationships. That makes as much sense as the lumberman who had no time to sharpen his axe because he was so busy felling trees.

It is time for a check-up. Let God's Word search us and God's Spirit bring healing to every dislocated joint. The kingdom must come, but that means a body *'joined and knit together'* so that *'each part is working properly'* (Ephesians 4:16 RSV).

Confronting one another

A father was about to apply 'the laying on of hands' to his small son for some misdemeanour, when the little lad bowed his head and prayed, 'For what we are about to receive may the Lord make us truly thankful'!

Whether or not he had had a sudden revelation of the blessing that comes from confrontation and discipline, it is certainly true that there *are* real blessings for the people of God through this means.

It was at the close of a convention meeting that a university student came to me for help. She had suffered a nervous breakdown. Although hers was a non-Christian home, she had been brought up by loving parents who gave her almost everything she wanted — everything, that is, except *correction*.

She told me that she had longed for them to set out guidelines for her — to tell her, for example, what time to be home at night. She had even longed for her dad to put her across his knee and spank her when she misbehaved. When I asked her about the effect of this lack of correction she replied, 'I felt very insecure.'

Confrontation is not simply for the blessing of security, but is an essential part of God's way to bring us into wholeness and maturity. That young student from an unbelieving home had rightly judged that her parents' correction would have been a mark of their love and commitment.

Father sets the pattern

God is the origin and perfect expression of all fatherhood, for in him, to quote Paul literally, *'all fatherhood in heaven and on earth is named'* (Ephesians 3:15). God's mercy and his judgment, his kindness and his sternness, are not contradictory but complementary expressions of his character. Judgment, as well as mercy, is an expression of his love.

Since we are *all* called to exercise a degree of authority in the family of God we must also learn how to confront and be confronted. It is one important way in which authority is exercised in the kingdom. In an age when there is such widespread rejection of authority in the world, and such fear of authoritarianism in the church, it is important that we allow our attitudes about this to be shaped by the Word of God and not by popular opinion.

'Admonish' is the word

The word 'confront' may not be found in the English New Testament, but we do have 'admonish' (or 'warn'), which is used to refer not only to public preaching and teaching but also to the task of personal correction.

'Admonish' is a shepherding word. In far too many churches, 'shepherding', if one calls it such, seems to have adopted the 'Little Bo Peep' philosophy. You will remember how the nursery rhyme goes:

> *Little Bo Peep has lost her sheep*
> *And doesn't know where to find them.*
> *Leave them alone and they'll come home,*
> *Wagging their tails behind them.*

But the truth is, sheep are sheep, not homing pigeons. They have the inborn tendency, not to come home, but to wander off! To a sheep, 'the grass grows greener on the other side of the fence'. That's why sheep need shepherds.

This tendency to wander is not confined to sheep of the 'woolly' variety — or perhaps we should say of the four-legged variety since so many of the two-legged variety also tend to be woolly! To Paul, admonishing was one of three major characteristics of the work of a shepherd. He says, 'Respect those who *work hard* among you, who are *over you* in the Lord and who *admonish* you' (1 Thessalonians 5:12).

What do we mean by authority?

One reason why much of what we are sharing here is a 'hard saying' to many Christians is because they do not understand authority.

In the kingdom of God all authority is *spiritual,* not legal. It cannot be enforced upon reluctant or unwilling subjects. For its effective exercise there must always be *relationship.* Knowledge of those who are over me must become the basis of love and trust — then I will be glad to honour them and submit to their shepherding care.

Where this relationship is lacking, the shepherding principle we are talking about breaks down. For their part, shepherds can only care for sheep who are submitted to them. Even God cannot shepherd those who are determined to rebel (Hosea 4:16).

All this emphasises *the importance of the local church's being a community of committed believers,* not a mixture of those who possess eternal life and those who merely profess to possess it. But it is not enough that they are the Lord's; they must also be committed to that body of believers and submitted to the authority of the leaders.

What is the purpose of shepherding?

The principle by which a human family is ruled is much the same as that which obtains in the family of God. This is why a father's inability to rule his own family disqualifies him from taking care of God's house (1 Timothy 3:4-5).

A father's aim in the correction of his children will be their maturing into responsible adulthood. At first a lot of correction is needed, but that will decrease as the child responds. It should hardly be necessary at all by the late teens. As correction succeeds it does itself out of a job!

It is just like this in the family of God. Though mature saints may need to be taught, directed and encouraged, they should but rarely need to be personally rebuked or corrected.

But remember, a believer may be a seasoned adult, and even many years on the Christian path, and still be a spiritual babe. As such he will only be able to cope with milk (Hebrews 5:12-14) — and will still need plenty of correction. The purpose of the shepherd will not change; it will always be the healing and wholeness of all the sheep, and their coming into full maturity where confrontation and correction are no longer necessary.

No simple answers

A good shepherd does not handle his sheep by rule of thumb but by shepherding wisdom according to their state and need. As well as confrontation and correction he will bring *directive counsel* that may be crucial for the developing of each one as well as for the good of the local body of believers. He will seek to channel each life into the most fruitful avenue of service.

Over the years I have been most grateful to brothers who have spoken into my life, not to deal with glaring sin, but to direct me into a new sphere of service, involving a new location. That kind of corrective counsel can be as difficult to give — and to receive — as that which is aimed at character deficiency.

A wise shepherd will sometimes refuse to bring any word of positive *direction,* but simply a word of *advice,* which the believer himself must weigh before coming to his own decision. For example, in response to a question about a business decision I would say, 'I'm not a businessman, but if you want my judgment I would say do so and so.' Notice how Paul sometimes gave his judgment rather than a definite injunction (1 Corinthians 7:25).

There was a wise elder to whom one of the flock constantly went for guidance on personal decisions. He had often given him guidance, but now realised that this man was not growing up. So one day he said to him, 'I'm not willing to counsel you on matters like this any more. You seek God for yourself, and come and tell me in a week's time what God has said to you.'

How far should a shepherd go?

Has a shepherd the right to tell a couple not to buy the lovely hi-fi equipment that they have set their hearts on? Does he have the right to break up exclusive boy/girl friendships in the church? Has he the right to ask a couple to submit their finances to the elders?

We have probably all heard the stories, plus embellishments, that have gone the rounds and produced reactions of indignation and criticism of the whole shepherding principle. Some, of course, are ridiculously exaggerated, but others, like the ones just mentioned, may be *substantially* true.

If you have committed your life to your leaders to shepherd you, then they not only have the right but a solemn charge and responsibility from God to speak into every area of your life which affects:

- ☐ your fellowship with God
- ☐ your walk and behaviour as a Christian
- ☐ your function in the church
- ☐ your witness before the world

If by your neglect of some truth or violation of some spiritual principle you are adversely affecting your own growth or the growth of others, then shepherds have a duty to speak. But let us fill in some background on these suggested cases, which may alter our initial judgment. And such cases are not fictitious or far-fetched; they represent nettles which are constantly having to be grasped by those in leadership.

The couple planning to buy the hi-fi have a history of financial mismanagement, are already over-committed with hire purchase and have other outstanding debts.

As for the boy/girl friendship, there has always been a question mark over Bill's commitment, both to Christ and to the church. Sue, on the other hand, had a wonderful conversion, but since she has been going out with Bill, she has lost her wholehearted love for Christ and both have become very erratic in their meeting with the church.

In such cases who would say that the shepherd should not speak?

In churches where these New Testament principles are applied, one would expect that major decisions, such as a couple becoming engaged, changing jobs, moving house (especially of moving out of the area) and all decisions which affect others in the church, would be referred as a matter of course to the elders for their prayerful consideration and counsel.

It is not a question of doing this under duress. In fact, most people, especially young couples, are most grateful for such counsel, for they know it may save them from the blunders they have seen others making. Sometimes it is simply a matter of timing, so that the counsel given is not 'no' but 'wait'. Impetuosity is a common fault with young Christians that shepherds have to correct.

The shepherd is accountable

It is because he is accountable that the shepherd is described as *'God's steward'* (Titus 1:7 RSV).

One day every shepherd will be required to give an account of the sheep committed to his care. 'Obey your leaders and submit to their authority. They keep watch over you as men who must give an account. Obey then so that their work will be a joy, not a burden, for that would be of no advantage to you' (Hebrews 13:17).

If for fear of 'rocking the boat' or of being accused of interfering or being authoritarian, or out of concern for their own popularity shepherds fail to confront and to admonish, they will suffer loss in that day when they render their account to God.

Though David was a great king, his record in this matter of confrontation was poor. We see it in his own family, in the cases of Amnon, Absalom and Adonijah (2 Samuel 13; 1 Kings 1:5-6). We see it in his failure to confront Joab, the captain of his army, for his murderous and treacherous behaviour on more than one occasion.

Because of this failure, David, on his death bed, had to call on his son Solomon to deal after his death with those things that he himself should have dealt with in life.

Not for elders only

It is significant that this command to admonish (Greek *noutheteo*) is as often laid on *God's people in general* as it is addressed to elders and leaders. Take these scriptures:

> 'I myself am convinced, my brothers, that you yourselves are full of goodness, complete in knowledge and competent to instruct [literally, to *admonish*] one another' (Romans 15:14).
>
> 'We urge you, brothers, warn [or *admonish*] those who are idle' (1 Thessalonians 5:14).
>
> 'If any one does not obey our instruction in this letter, take special note of him. Do not associate with him, in order that he may feel ashamed. Yet do not regard him as an enemy, but warn [or *admonish*] him as a brother' (2 Thessalonians 3:14-15).

So we are *all* involved in the admonishing business. It won't always mean rebuking or correcting, though it will require that at times. If we were more diligent in this, what a burden we would lift from the shoulders of our leaders. They could concentrate on the admonishing that only elders can do.

When Jesus said to his disciples, 'If your brother sins against you, go and show him his fault, just between the two of you' (Matthew 18:15-20; see also Luke 17:3-4), he was teaching them nothing less than *personal confrontation.*

But how seldom do we really obey it? It is often the case that the person we ought to confront has wounded us, and we don't particularly *want* reconciliation. We are more concerned about nursing our hurt feelings than either obeying Christ's command or seeing our brother restored.

How true are Bob Mumford's words: 'When we don't confront our brothers, we are rejecting them.'

How do you confront?

Jesus said that if you confront your brother and he listens to you, 'You have won your brother over.'

This gives us the motive for confronting and provides the first answer to our question. You confront *with a right motive.* Not to humiliate him, not to put him in his place or give him a piece of your mind, but to win him back — back to Christ and to you! It's the brother's restoration, not your vindication, that is your motive.

In other words, admonishing must be done *with love* — a love that is 'not self-seeking'. We find that Paul admonished with tears (Acts 20:19-21). The absence of compassion is the major reason for the occasional failure of confrontation to bring about reconciliation. It can even result in a widening of the breach.

Then you must do it *'gently'* (NIV), or as the older versions have it, with a *'spirit of meekness'* (Galatians 6:1; 1 Corinthians 4:21).

Meekness is not weakness, but strength under control. It means keeping your emotions in check, so you do not come over harshly or with undue strength — 'I'm going to hurt him because he hurt me.' If it's my pride that has been hurt, the need for a spirit of meekness before I tackle my brother is even greater. Pride will make the encounter most unlikely to result in true reconciliation.

You must also do it *in faith.* If you go to your brother in fear that your efforts will misfire, or not believing that he will receive what you say — 'He'll never change' — then it will very likely become a fulfilment of the 'reverse version': 'According to your unbelief be it unto you'!

Finally, you must do it *with perseverance.* You don't give up after the first attempt. Jesus told us what we were to do if the first attempt did not succeed. Take *one or two others* along with you and try again. Those one or two others will be able to listen to you both and speak into the situation impartially. You may feel that you are so right, but you too may need help if your attitudes and reactions need adjusting.

If even this does not have the desired effect, the final court of appeal is *the church* itself. And if he refuses to heed the voice of the church he has to be treated as an outsider. The censure of the whole church will then become a godly pressure to bring about repentance.

But how seldom is confrontation pressed through to this point! If the first effort fails, people tend to give up. Little wonder the church is littered with longstanding broken relationships.

Inheritance at stake

It's often said, 'Only those *under* authority *have* authority!' It is equally true that only those who have learned to *receive* correction are qualified to *give* it.

This is where we have to begin. Have you realised that receiving the discipline of correction, whether direct from God or through others, is a proof of your sonship? On the other side of the coin, Scripture insists, 'If you are not disciplined . . . then you are illegitimate children and not true sons' (Hebrews 12:8).

What God is saying here is that if you reject discipline you reject the blessing of sonship. You are actually putting your inheritance at risk. Illegitimate sons do not inherit.

The Israelites in the wilderness were God's redeemed people but they failed to respond to the command and correction of Moses, the shepherd God had set over them. It cost them their inheritance; they never made it to Canaan.

Let no-one say, 'That's all old covenant stuff. We are under grace.' Listen to Paul: 'These things happened to them [the Israelites in the wilderness] as examples and were written down as warnings for us' (1 Corinthians 10:11).

In the same epistle he warns sinning believers in the Corinthian church, enriched though they were with spiritual gifts, that they could not continue in their unrighteousness and expect to inherit the kingdom of God (1 Corinthians 6:9-10).

Let us, then, joyfully submit to spiritual confrontation and correction, through whatever channel it may come, so that we may receive one day 'the reward of the inheritance'.

The city vision

Before God appeared to him, Abraham was no wandering Bedouin but a sophisticated city-dweller, belonging to a community where art and architecture were highly developed, and the educated could not only read and write, but even work out square and cube roots. Not bad for the twentieth century BC!

It was the 'city' concept that had always dominated Abraham's thinking, but when 'the God of glory' appeared to him he caught a vision of another city — one with the glorious qualities he had found sadly lacking in the city of his birth.

It was this vision that was to motivate him all his days. He abandoned the one in search of the other. Having seen the city of God he could not settle for the city of Ur. The choice that faced Abraham four thousand years ago faces us today.

We need to remember that behind the faith, obedience and spirit of adventure that marked Abraham's life was his vision of this city. Through setbacks, domestic problems, lapses of faith and a gigantic exercise in patience, Abraham kept going. He did not waver. He never returned to his native land, though he had opportunity. He did not veer to his right or left. And all because he had caught the vision of a city.

But he was no mere dreamer or visionary, for 'faith is being sure of what we hope for and certain of what we do not see'.

In Revelation John sees the eternal city 'coming down from God out of heaven'. That emphasises its heavenly origin. 'It shone with the glory of God' — it expressed the very character of God, whose dwelling-place it was. It was 'like a jasper, clear as crystal' — it had nothing to hide but everything to display.

We read that 'anyone who does what is shameful or deceitful' is debarred. For that reason, 'it had a great high wall', too high to be scaled. So this was no easy come, easy go, free-for-all community. The boundary lines were clearly drawn. You could only get in through the appointed gates.

Finally, we see the city as the greatest and most influential element in the universe, with the nations walking by its light and the kings of the earth bringing their splendour into it. Its citizens live in the unending day of God's glory, the light that streams from the Lamb.

But how do we reconcile this city, with its divine rule and order, its heavenly purity and unity, with what goes for the community of God around us? It is clear that the professing church bears little or no resemblance to the heavenly blueprint.

'There is no prospect of seeing the mess sorted out till Jesus comes back,' many will be quick to tell us. Is that really God's verdict? Or are we being ruled in our thinking by what we see around us rather than by what God says in his Word?

This is no hypothetical question. We are touching one of the greatest hindrances to the fulfilment of God's purposes in the earth, that is, an attitude of incredulity that defers to another age what God wants to fulfil in this one. And so we settle now for something which falls far short of what God intends. Those who do so are not being gripped by the vision of the city.

Has the Bible an answer to those who so futurise the vision that it calls for no radical and practical response in the here and now?

Early on in Revelation, in the letter Jesus sent to the church in Philadelphia, he promises to the one who overcomes that he will write on him 'the name of the city of my God, the new Jerusalem, which *is coming down* out of heaven from my God'. Notice the present continuous tense. The coming down is not only a future event, but a present process. It's happening now.

We sing about marching to Zion, but it is equally true that 'You *have come* to Mount Zion, to the heavenly Jerusalem, the city of the living God.' Zion is a present as well as a future reality.

To relegate it all to 'the sweet by-and-by' and thus avoid facing up to 'the nasty now-and-now' is a cop-out! But if you are gripped by the vision of the city you can never settle for anything less. It will affect how you labour, how you build, how you pray, how you relate with those who share that vision and with those who don't.

If you have never had that vision, or if you have lost it or allowed it to become fuzzy, ask God to anoint your eyes with the ointment of his Spirit. 'Call to me,' he says, 'and I will answer you and tell you great and unsearchable things you do not know.'

God's purposes are ripening fast. The city is coming down. It's time to embrace it.

A praying church

We are indebted to Dr Luke for the pen portrait of 'the praying Christ' that emerges in his gospel narrative. Seven times he tells us that Jesus prayed, covering the major crises in the life of our Lord.

It is not surprising, therefore, that the same writer, in his history of the early church commonly called 'the Acts', has presented to us the picture of 'the praying church'. The disciples had learned from the Master, and now the body is imitating the Head. We see them coming through one crisis after another — on their knees.

J.B. Phillips, translating the Acts, tells how he found the story of 'the young church' profoundly disturbing.

'This surely is *the church as it was meant to be,'* he commented. 'It is vigorous and flexible, for these are the days before it ever became fat and short of breath through prosperity, or muscle-bound by over-organisation. These men did not make "acts of faith"; they believed. They did not "say their prayers"; they really prayed. They did not hold conferences on psychosomatic medicine; they simply healed the sick. But if they were uncomplicated and naïve by modern standards we have ruefully to admit that they were *open on the Godward side* in a way that is almost unknown today.'

This openness to God was one of the obvious secrets of their huge success. Their belief in a transcendent God, that is, a God exalted above and distinct from his universe, did not prevent them believing in an immanent God, that is, one who permeated his universe, and who could be expected to manifest his presence and power on their behalf at any time. They were obviously at home in the supernatural. They prayed and expected him to intervene on their behalf — and he did.

When we move from the narrative of the gospels to that of the Acts, we find the emphasis shifts from personal praying to corporate praying.

It is not that there is no individual praying in the Acts record

— far from it; but with the coming of the Spirit the disciples had found for the first time a corporate identity. Almost overnight they had become 'bodywise' in their thinking. *Koinonia* (the shared life, fellowship) was a sparkling new gem in their spiritual treasury.

Had not Jesus taught them, 'If two of you on earth agree about anything you ask for, it will be done' (Matthew 18:19)? Now they were experiencing it. They were discovering that there was a power generated by a union of prayer, beyond anything that could be achieved by the sum total of their individual efforts.

The crisis of inauguration

The opening chapter of the Acts introduces us to a church born out of the womb of prayer, that in turn became a praying church. After our Lord's return to heaven, his disciples withdrew to the upper room in obedience to his parting counsel, to stay in the city of Jerusalem and wait for the Holy Spirit.

'All these with one accord devoted themselves to prayer' (Acts 1:14 RSV). It would no doubt have been very instructive could we have put an ear to the keyhole during those ten days of waiting. Although Scripture does not enlighten us, we may safely assume that there was *progression* in their praying.

At first we would have sensed a very necessary negative strain running through their prayers. Only weeks before, they had been quarrelling as to who should be the greatest in the kingdom. Still fresh in their minds, like an unhealed wound, would be the memory of that hour of their Master's greatest need, when they had all forsaken him and run like frightened rabbits to their holes. There would have been some very humble prayers of confession.

From time to time a disciple would pick his way through the standing, kneeling or prone figures, to find some estranged brother or sister. A few whispered words, the mingling of tears, the embrace of reconciliation, and another wound in 'the body' had been healed. Before they could 'agree together' they must be truly one in spirit.

Then, as the days passed by, they would begin to forget the things that were behind and reach forward to what lay before. Confession was now being replaced by intercession.

They would remind the Lord of his promise: 'You said, "How much more will your heavenly Father give the Holy Spirit to those who ask him." You said, "Stay in the city until you are clothed with power from on high." You said, "Before many days you shall be baptised in the Holy Spirit."'

Their prayers were now characterised by a new spirit of faith and fervour. 'Lord, we believe your word. Do for us what you have promised.' Out of this union of believing prayer some would break through into praise and thanksgiving. They were now certain that the answer was on the way. It came on the day of Pentecost.

Today most people are being baptised in the Spirit by personal reception through the laying on of hands, as did Saul of Tarsus, rather than through a corporate outpouring, as at Pentecost. But God has surely a bigger thing in store than anything we are witnessing in Britain through the charismatic movement.

There is an outpouring of the Spirit, in fulfilment of the prophecy of Joel (2:28-29), that comes like an earthquake, finding its epicentre in the church and sending its shock waves radiating out into the secular community. That kind of visitation is heaven's response to the kind of praying that took place in the upper room. It is time for us to seek the Lord for this.

The crisis of consolidation

Every great thrust of the Spirit, if it is to have any lasting effect, must be followed by consolidation, and Pentecost was no exception.

What that involved is described for us in Acts 2:41-47. Among other things we are told that this young church devoted themselves to *prayer* (v42). This expression, 'devoted themselves' or 'continued steadfastly in', is the same as Luke uses to describe their pre-Pentecost praying (1:14). The inner core of the church had spent ten days in prayer, a long enough prayer meeting by any standards. They had received their answer on the day of Pentecost. Now surely they could let up and give prayer a rest for a while? Not a bit. They 'devoted themselves' to it, along with the new converts.

Here then is an obvious reason why this movement went from strength to strength when other revivals have quickly petered out. 'From the day of Pentecost,' wrote Dr A.T. Pierson, 'there has been not one great spiritual awakening in any land which has not begun in a union of prayer, though only among two or three; no such outward, upward movement has continued after such prayer meetings have declined.'

It is when the first wave of a movement has spent itself that the people of God are tempted to settle down and enjoy the spoil. An air of self-satisfaction and complacency creeps in. It is then that the work is most vulnerable to the counter-attacks of the devil.

Success in the work of the kingdom is so much a question of getting one's priorities right. If administration is neglected there is an immediate outcry, but you can neglect prayer and get away with it — for a while. In the end, however, you are left with the form without the power.

In a later crisis (Acts 6:1-4) we see how the apostles handled this temptation, and ensured the progress of the work. Here, right at the beginning, the fact that 'they devoted themselves . . . to prayer' suggests that they gave place and priority to this, alongside teaching, fellowship and breaking of bread. This consolidated the ground gained, and prepared the way for the next thrust.

Paul uses the same word when he says, '*Devote* yourselves to prayer, being watchful and thankful' (Colossians 4:2). I'm sure the praying of the early church was punctuated with much thanksgiving, as they praised God for all he had done and was continuing to do. It was also accompanied by watchfulness, for they well knew that the coming of Pentecost did not mean that the devil had been put out of business.

Because, in the past, so much prayer has tended to be legalistic, there has been a tendency to play it down, both personal and corporate, and to stress other new and more exciting aspects of church life. We need to look afresh at our priorities, and then to God, that we may experience a new spirit of prayer, such as characterised those first Christians. This will be a delight rather than a duty, and because it is in the plan of God it will be in the flow of the Spirit.

The crisis of opposition

Pentecost had taken Jerusalem by storm. But now the young church was to feel the inevitable reaction of the religious hierarchy.

The healing of the lame man at the temple gate gave Peter another great evangelistic opportunity. But the religious leaders were quick to react, too. Before Peter's sermon was through they had arrested him and John, and brought them before the Sanhedrin. In the end they threatened them and let them go.

When the two apostles reported to their fellow-believers what had transpired, there was a spontaneous and united outburst of supernatural praying, all using the same words (Acts 4:24-30).

Their prayer is a God-given model. They did not begin with the problem, they began with God, as the 'Sovereign Lord', Creator of the universe.

This cut the opposition down to size. The threatenings of their rulers were futile. Their plottings would only fulfil what God had predetermined. There were no prayers for protection or escape. They were not on the defensive, but on the attack! Sanhedrin or no Sanhedrin, they would take the city for God.

In the end they only asked for two things. First, 'Take care of these threatenings and enable us to continue to speak your word with boldness.' Second, 'Confirm that word by healings, by signs and by wonders.' In other words, 'You give us grace to do our part, while you do your part, and together we'll take the kingdom by storm.'

Little wonder the building shook — that was God saying 'Amen', and assuring them that he would shake the opposition to its very foundations. Filled afresh with the Holy Spirit, they continued to speak with all boldness.

I am expecting God to wind up this age of grace as he began it. The prophetic word warns us of opposition and persecution (Luke 21:12). In the teeth of this there will be, immediately prior to Christ's return, the worldwide proclamation of the gospel of the kingdom (Matthew 24:14). This message will be confirmed by signs and wonders, just as it was when preached by Christ and his apostles (Hebrews 2:3-4).

Jesus described the wind-up of the age as 'the time of harvest' (Matthew 13:30, 39), not 'the time of dearth'. The age is to end in triumph, not tragedy.

It is not too much to believe that God will give to his people in these days the same spirit of prayer that he gave to those early Christians, for they were men of like passions as us. Then the mightier working of God will overcome all opposition, and the saints of the Most High will take the kingdom.

God, make us a praying church!

Deception — Satan's deadliest weapon

He was a spiritual pioneer. Well before the charismatic renewal he was moving in the things of the Spirit and, through his writings, setting forth many of the truths of renewal and restoration. It was quite a thrill to find we spoke the same language.

What a shock, some years after our brief acquaintance, to learn that he had left his wife after developing an infatuation for his secretary.

Close friends had reasoned with him, all to no avail. He had his 'legitimate' reasons: there was incompatibility and now he had found a true mate with whom he could be spiritually one. He soon left the ministry he had been involved with and I have never heard of him since.

In almost all such cases there is a work of deception. Invariably he (or she) tries to justify the sin or the error. 'Woe to those who call evil good and good evil, who put darkness for light and light for darkness' (Isaiah 5:20).

We have all been 'suckers' for Satan's deceptive work. We were born into the kingdom of Satan, held captive with deceptive chains of darkness. We had eyes, but we could not see; ears, but we could not hear. Many falsehoods were fed us and we received them as truth, and many truths were presented to us as falsehoods. It was only the grace of God that freed us from our darkness and brought us into light.

Three varieties

Deception is the act of representing as true what is known to be false, or representing as false what is known to be true. Those who fall for either ruse are said to be deceived.

One of the most common instruments of deception is lying. Satan is described by Jesus as 'the father of lies' (John 8:44) and as the one who deceives, or leads astray, the whole world (Revelation 12:9).

Not all deception is a direct work of Satan, though he is always waiting to use the occasion for his advantage. Deception may take three forms. There is *satanic deception,* by the direct action of Satan or his demons. There is *human deception* by those who are the human agents of Satan. And there is *self-deception.* Let us look for a moment at the originator and architect of it all.

The deceiver deceived

Satan was evidently a supreme angel serving in God's presence, until cast down from heaven because of his rebellion. What was he after? 'I will raise my throne above the stars [angels] of God . . . I will make myself like the Most High' (Isaiah 14:13-14). His aim: a leap upward to become God. His fate: a disastrous downward fall to eternal ruin.

Since Satan is no fool, he must have believed he could succeed. In this conviction he was totally deceived — *self-deceived.* So the one who initiated all deception commenced it by being deceived himself!

A large number of angels were the first victims of Satan's deceptive tactics. These 'stars' (angels) 'swept . . . out of the sky' (Revelation 12:4) by Satan were his first victims. But he soon turned his attention to the newly created earth and to man, the masterpiece of God's creative genius.

The earth infected

Satan drew and engaged Eve with a provocative question: 'Did God really say . . . ?', creating doubt and uncertainty. Then, when her guard was down, he let loose the knockout blow, denying God's plain statement that they would die if they ate of the forbidden fruit. God had an ulterior motive, he suggested: he was denying them the right to be gods themselves (Genesis 3).

Before we criticise Mrs Adam for being so gullible, let me ask you a question. Have you ever had a season of backsliding, a time of coldness or lukewarmness, when other interests drew you away from your devotion to Christ? If so, you have been beguiled just like Eve!

'I am afraid,' wrote Paul, 'that just as Eve was deceived by the serpent's cunning, *your* minds may somehow be led astray from your sincere and pure devotion to Christ' (2 Corinthians 11:3).

How did it happen? Satan deceived us into thinking that our material interests, desire for worldly pleasure, popularity or some other form of self-seeking, had more to offer than seeking the kingdom of God, and for a while we believed his lie.

Deceiving agents

There is much warning in Scripture about this second form — human deception. Jesus told us, 'Watch out for false prophets. They come to you in sheep's clothing, but inwardly they are ferocious wolves. By their fruit you will recognise them' (Matthew 7:15-16).

Not by their gift or their charisma, but by their *fruit.* Indeed, Jesus went on to say that on the coming day of judgment many would say to him, 'Lord, Lord, did we not prophesy in your name, and in your name drive out demons and perform many miracles?' (v22). But he would have to reply, 'I never knew you. Away from me, you evildoers!' (v23).

So the test would not be performance, display of power or any charismatic manifestation, but *the fruit of Christian character,* the likeness of Jesus in the individual.

In an overseas situation a few of us had met to pray and confer over a coming conference. We were startled by a prophecy that warned us that one would come in the guise of a prophet and seek to bring a word, but that he was not of God's Spirit. We would not recognise him by seeing with the eye or hearing with the ear, but because he did not have God's love in his heart.

At the conference we kept our eyes skinned, but no-one showed up to fit the description. In fact, he was already moving in the new charismatic circles that had sprung up in that country. He had striking insights, words of knowledge, and many were being dazzled by his charismatic gifts.

'I am Elijah'

In the end we were alerted as to who this man might be, and it fell to my lot to test the spirit (1 John 4:1-3).

The challenge brought a dramatic response. He stormed up and down the room, pronouncing a curse on me and telling me to prepare to meet my God. I experienced a numbing pain in my spine (which I am glad to say passed away in a few minutes). He kept shouting out that he was the great prophet Elijah who was to come before the day of the Lord. It was very clear that we had uncovered the man 'who did not have the love of God in his heart'!

Paul warned against 'false apostles, deceitful workmen, masquerading as apostles of Christ'. And no wonder, for Satan himself masquerades as 'an angel of light' (2 Corinthians 11:13-14). They were on the scene in Paul's day. They are on the scene today, and will be to the end of the age.

Self-deception

Paul warns us of the common malaise called self-deception. He said — possibly with a twinkle in his eye — 'If anyone thinks he is something when he is nothing, *he deceives himself*' (Galatians 6:3). This is not unrelated to the very first case of self-deception, which we saw came about through the pride of Satan.

Mr Bighead will always be a good candidate for self-deception. Here is the antidote: 'By the grace given me I say to every one of you: Do not think of yourself more highly than you ought, but rather think of yourself with sober judgment, in accordance with the measure of faith God has given you' (Romans 12:3).

Paul has a second warning for the Galatians regarding self-deception. 'Do not be deceived,' he says. 'God cannot be mocked. A man reaps what he sows' (Galatians 6:7).

There is many a Christian today living under the illusion that through grace he can live as he likes, 'to please his sinful nature', and still reap the blessing of God. No way, says Paul. You reap according to your sowing, and that means if you sow to the flesh you reap destruction.

Hearing without doing

Just as common is the illusion that you can happily sit under the ministry of God's word and be blessed by it, even though you do nothing about obeying it.

James would bring us down with a godly bump. He says, 'Do not merely listen to the word, and so *deceive yourselves*. Do what it says. Anyone who listens to the word but does not do what it says is like a man who looks at his face in a mirror and, after looking at himself, goes away and immediately forgets what he looks like' (James 1:22-24).

There is no blessing whatever in hearing the word if we do not obey it. In fact, the very reverse is the case. The more we hear, the more responsible we become. 'From everyone who has been given much [for example, through teaching], much will be demanded' (Luke 12:48).

Again, 'If anyone considers himself religious and yet does not keep a tight rein on his tongue, *he deceives himself* and his religion is worthless.'

You can find this gentleman in most Christian circles. He adopts a spiritual pose, has lots to say that seems spiritual, but his tongue is undisciplined and he is entirely deceived as to his spiritual state. God says his 'spirituality' is 'worthless'!

Before leaving this area of self-deception there is one form of it that we must look at more fully.

Soul and spirit

As Christians we can live 'according to the sinful nature' or we can live 'according to the Spirit' (Romans 8:4). Paul had to rebuke the Corinthians because they were carnal (or soulish) rather than spiritual (1 Corinthians 3:1). Jesus described the Spirit-filled life as the flowing out from our inner man of rivers of living water. It is the work of the Holy Spirit, not of human effort.

Years ago I was preaching in London during a time of widespread power cuts. Just as the meeting was getting under way the power was cut off and the staff switched to the building's own battery-operated supply. Alas, this got progressively dimmer, and I eventually rose to speak in almost total darkness.

The hall's own power supply was pathetic in comparison with a normal mains supply. With God, the power is never cut off, but *we can still switch to our own feeble resources.*

This is what happened to the Galatians. 'Are you so foolish?' asked Paul. 'After beginning with the Spirit, are you now trying to obtain your goal by human effort?' (Galatians 3:3).

By switching to their own 'battery supply', the Galatians had cut themselves off from the mighty resources of heaven's power station — and they were totally oblivious of what had taken place! Here were believers who had been filled with the Spirit in the early days of their Christian life. They had seen God move in supernatural power. And now they were turning back to these 'weak and beggarly elements' of natural resources.

No wonder Paul asks if they had been bewitched!

Another power

What is the nature of the power that keeps the wheels of *your* Christian life turning? Is it soulish or is it spiritual? Is it the power of personality or self-effort, or is it the power of the Holy Spirit? The tragic lesson of the Galatians is that you can begin with the latter, and then end up with the former, *and be totally unaware that you have made the switch.*

It is sadly possible to have ambition and aspiration in our Christian life which is soulish (finding its source in ourselves rather than in God) and not spiritual. There is a zeal for God which is without knowledge. It may well impress others, but it does not impress God.

Two priests once died before God for offering 'strange fire' on God's altar (Numbers 3:2-4). We need to have the fire burning within, but it must be God-lit and God-sustained. The measure in which we do our praying, giving and fasting to impress others is the measure in which we fail to impress God.

Setting captives free

What is commonly called 'deliverance ministry' (setting people free from the power of Satan) is a fruitful field for satanic deception.

Without question there is an authentic New Testament ministry of breaking the hold of Satan in human lives. But where believers try to operate this without reference to the guidelines and safeguards of the New Testament, they are in great danger of being deceived.

In a charismatic church of my acquaintance a young woman, who had been converted and filled with the Spirit, became involved with the pastor and his wife in 'deliverance ministry'. This young woman was, we were informed, able to attract to herself, during meetings, evil spirits from those whom she discerned to be troubled by them. When the meeting was over she would have these cast out by the pastor. In this way people were ostensibly 'delivered' from demon power.

Of course, it was all a big deception. There is nothing remotely like this in the New Testament.

Counterfeit

Visiting Wales, I was invited to counsel a young woman in spiritual difficulty. It was suggested that she needed deliverance. Praying over the matter beforehand, I became convinced that demons were not involved.

After counselling her, I commenced to pray. Immediately 'the enemy' began to manifest himself. There were strange movements and contortions that I had often seen before in times of deliverance. I stopped praying and said to the young woman, 'I'm not going to try to set you free from demons you haven't got!'

The young lady looked at me in wide-eyed astonishment. I continued praying, but there were no more manifestations. She was not actively trying to deceive me. She herself had been deceived into thinking that she was 'possessed' and was *unconsciously* simulating the symptoms she had seen in others.

Jesus is our guide

In this vital area the ministry of Christ provides us with all the guidelines we need. To set people free from demonic power he seldom needed to identify or name the demon, and certainly not to demand that the demon name itself. That happened only once.

Jesus never went in for prolonged deliverance sessions, and the setting free of a person from more than one demon was extremely rare. Mary Magdalene, 'from whom seven demons had come out', is mentioned only because her case was remarkable and exceptional. The Gadarene demoniac, so often quoted as justification for casting innumerable demons out of a person, in fact only involved for Jesus the exorcism of *one* spirit (Mark 5:2-8).

When we hear some enthusiast reporting, 'We cast twenty-three demons out of him, and we plan to deal with the rest next time!' we may suspect that Satan is at his deceptive tricks again. It is vital that we subject the apparent evidence of our outward senses to the touchstone of God's Word. Otherwise we become gullible and easy victims of Satan's subtle devices.

It is worth noting, too, that the deliverance ministry of Jesus was almost exclusively among the multitudes, and not within his growing band of committed disciples. Similarly with the apostles. We don't find them casting out spirits in the church, but in connection with their evangelistic activity.

Food for thought

Here are a few guidelines worthy of consideration regarding deliverance:

- ☐ We should expect that our experiences and our practices should fall broadly within the examples given us in the New Testament
- ☐ We do not find in the New Testament any servant of God who was a specialist in deliverance, nor were there any deliverance centres
- ☐ No servant of God used in this way was a solo performer. They worked in pairs or teams
- ☐ A spiritual understanding of the armour of God (Ephesians 6) and its appropriation is vital in this area
- ☐ Essential equipment for this ministry involves authentic gifts of the Spirit in faith, words of knowledge and the discerning of spirits

Who is to blame?

If a person becomes a victim of Satan's wiles, will not Satan be held accountable rather than the person? The fact is that no-one is an innocent victim of deception. He cannot 'pass the buck', as that first pair tried to do in the garden.

Whether the deception comes direct from Satan, through Satan's agents or is a case of self-deception, *God holds the person deceived responsible.* There has been a violation of a divine principle. Or disobedience to the Word of God. Or a refusal to face reality. There are always attitudes of heart that have laid one open to the deception.

Just before he went to the cross Jesus said to his disciples, 'The prince of this world is coming. He has no hold on me' (John 14:30). In other words, there was no avenue along which Satan could attack him, no landing-strip on which he could alight. Jesus had not laid himself open to the enemy.

Safety in humility

What was it that led to Satan being deceived and thus becoming the deceiver? It was the *pride* and *rebellion* of his own heart. Wherever these two evils are found among God's people, there, you can be sure, the deceiver will be at work, and often those involved will not be open to reason or entreaty.

Your sure protection is to 'clothe yourselves with humility towards one another, because, "God opposes the proud but gives grace to the humble." Humble yourselves, therefore, under God's mighty hand' (1 Peter 5:5-6).

It is the humble person, nestling under God's mighty hand, who is protected. He will recognise the importance of those who are over him and their counsel. He will also see the value of those alongside him. Both are part of his protection. He will avoid the proud, independent spirit that makes it easy for the enemy sniper to pick him off.

What of the future?

The work of deception that brought about the fall of that first pair in the garden, and which has continued down the centuries, is not going to go away. In fact, as both the church and the spirit of iniquity in the world come to their full fruition we may expect a dramatic increase in this form of satanic activity.

Our Lord Jesus predicted this, and so did his apostles. Our Lord warned that false Christs and false prophets would arise, who 'will appear and perform great signs and miracles to deceive even the elect — if that were possible' (Matthew 24:24).

Paul warned of the coming of the man of sin, or 'the lawless one . . . displayed in all kinds of counterfeit miracles, signs and wonders, and in every sort of evil that deceives those who are perishing. They perish because they refused to love the truth and so be saved' (2 Thessalonians 2:9-10).

The victims of this deceptive work will be the unsaved, who 'perish because they refused to love the truth'. But our Lord's words about the signs and miracles that might 'deceive even the elect — if that were possible' clearly hold out the possibility that some believers may be deceived.

Stay safe!

There is nothing here to suggest that the deceptive work of Satan is going to *prevail* among God's people. Jesus is coming back for a glorious bride, not for a poor woman seduced and deceived by the wiles of the enemy.

Now is the time to heed the warnings of Scripture, so that we are not ignorant of Satan's devices. Now is the time to humble ourselves under God's mighty hand and to resist the devil, that he may flee from us.

We *must not* and we *need not* be casualties of the end-time conflict. Instead, let us determine to stand our ground and remain as victors on the field of battle.

What kind of God do we believe in?

A God whose decrees are infallible, whose will is irresistible, who brooks no rival, who overturns every power, heavenly or earthly, that withstands his purpose — is this really the God of the Bible?

It is a far cry from the popular image of a heavenly Santa Claus who smiles down upon his creation from some vantage-point in outer space, but never dreams of lifting a finger to interfere in its affairs.

To people of the world the truth of a sovereign God is an awesome and fearful concept from which they shrink. Others cannot reconcile that man is a free moral agent with the concept of a God who 'does as he pleases with the powers of heaven and the peoples of the earth. No-one can hold back his hand or say to him, "What have you done?"' They seem to think that when the Almighty invested man with free will he automatically abdicated the throne of his universe in man's favour.

It is the conflict between God's sovereign will and man's freedom of choice that lies at the heart of the age-old Calvinist-Arminian controversy. It is not our purpose here to try to reconcile conflicting viewpoints that have baffled some of the greatest theologians over the centuries. We shall take a practical, even simplistic, approach, though one that we believe is wholly biblical.

We shall never shrink from the truth of divine sovereignty provided we think of it as absolute power in the hands of absolute goodness. Rather will we thrill at every revelation of such a God as we meet him in Scripture and in experience. Once captivated by the truth that such a God rules the universe, the effects upon us are profound. Let us consider some of them.

It is an *antidote to the malaise of self-rejection* from which so many Christians suffer, for it reminds us that we are his workmanship.

He has created us the way we are, our physical appearance, mental capacity, our gifts and talents, natural strengths and weaknesses — all are expressions of his sovereign will, and he makes no mistakes. In the light of this, our attitude of self-rejection is nothing short of rebellion. He wanted us this way, but we wanted something different.

There is nothing for it but to repent of our rebellion, joyfully embrace the will of God, and declare from the heart, 'Thank you, God, for making me me.'

The truth of election, that we were chosen in Christ before the world was, is another expression of divine sovereignty. This truth ministers healing to those whose self-rejection springs from the knowledge that they were born out of wedlock. They carry a deep scar on their spirits because they believe they are the product of sin and that their lives are for ever blighted in consequence.

Let's get it straight: there are no illegitimate children — only illegitimate parents! It is God who gives conception and birth.

You, who carry this kind of inner hurt, are just as much his workmanship as any other of his children. Before the act took place that gave you existence, you were 'chosen according to the foreknowledge of God'. So he knew beforehand all about the circumstances, and they did not alter his choice.

He has not made do with you because he had no other. Of the millions he might have chosen with no such birth stigma, he has chosen you to be an object of his special love and grace. He points to your election to let you know that you are special.

The truth of God's sovereignty is a source of immense comfort because it *lifts us above our adverse circumstances.* We cannot be simply victims of change, targets for Satan or easy game for the malign intentions of our fellow-men. At all times we are under the benevolent government of an omnipotent God.

He also rules Satan, evil men and all the circumstances of life. He is totally committed to our good and has absolute power to ensure that his will is done. 'He holds you and me in his hands.'

Of course, this does not mean immunity from the winds of sorrow or adversity, but it does mean that these are as much under his control and turned for our good as when he makes our sea a calm. Romans 8:28 holds true. Come what may, all is well if our God reigns.

Divine sovereignty is also a *great faith sustainer and faith builder.* It is the infallible guarantee that lies behind every promise God has uttered. Given the fulfilment of the conditions, the fulfilment of the promise is as certain as tomorrow's dawn. 'God is not a man that he should lie, nor a son of man, that he should change his mind. Does he speak and then not act? Does he promise and not fulfil?'

Think back to that promise God so clearly gave you, which for some reason still awaits fulfilment. He has not changed his mind about it, even if you have changed yours. He is as ready to fulfil it now as when he first uttered it, if you will but believe and obey.

Not least, God's sovereignty is *the ground of our hope.* It makes us incorrigible optimists. It removes all doubt about the final outcome of the conflict. We *know* we are on the winning side. We *know* that every knee will bow and every tongue confess. We *know* that the kingdom of this world will soon become the kingdom of our God and of his Christ, and that he will reign for ever and ever.

In the heat of battle, with our backs to the wall, we can lift up our heads because we know that 'God omnipotent reigns'.

God has spoken

The maternity ward, the children's playground and the football stadium bear witness to the fact that at every stage of his development man is highly vocal.

Is it conceivable that the God who created him is inarticulate? Yet that is what many otherwise intelligent people are ready to assume. Their concept of God seems to rise no higher than 'the man upstairs' who looks down benignly (and, it would seem, helplessly) on the universe he has created. Having set it all in motion, and handed it over to man, he is apparently unwilling or unable to speak into it, or to influence its course in any way.

Or perhaps he didn't create it at all. Perhaps, by 'a fortuitous concourse of atoms' it came to be — and the Almighty is still recovering from the shock!

He spoke through the prophets

The moment we open our Bible we are introduced to a God who has been speaking consistently since the beginning of time. At his command the world sprang into being and by his word of power it is upheld.

From the moment God gave man dominion over the works he had made he has been communicating with him. He spoke directly to the first pair in the garden, and in the centuries that followed he clothed men and women with his Spirit so that they became his mouthpiece to the people. 'Men spake from God as they were carried along by the Holy Spirit.' 'God spoke to our forefathers through the prophets.'

He spoke in his Son

Then it seemed as though God gathered it all up to express himself in one final, all-inclusive declaration — in his Son, the living Word, the mind of God told out, the heart of God laid bare, the radiance of his glory and the stamp of his very being.

If you like, the Son was God's last Word. In him God spoke it all. And having spoken it, he had nothing more to say. All further utterance was but the elaboration of that one final Word.

How man responds to that Word, either in submission — 'My Lord and my God' — or in rebellion — 'I will not have this man to reign' — determines his destiny.

The object of the written Word

Jesus loved and reverenced the written Word, and by the way he used it against Satan in the wilderness temptation we see how he had let that Word saturate his mind and fill his heart.

'These are the Scriptures that testify about me,' he once said. And on that famous walk to Emmaus with two of his disciples, 'he explained to them what was said *in all the Scriptures* concerning himself'. This tells us that the supreme purpose of the written Word is to reveal the living Word, and that is not a once-for-all operation.

Need we bother?

If by faith we have received the living Word, and God has sent his Spirit into our hearts, need we bother about the Scriptures?

'Just walk by faith,' some would tell us, 'and enjoy a spontaneous expression of your new life in Jesus. Don't get into bondage over Bible reading. Read it as and when you feel like it. Remember, "the letter kills, but the Spirit gives life". God has many ways of speaking to us.'

Though there is some truth here, the effect of such thinking in the long term is to instil a *laissez-faire* attitude to the Scriptures which is spiritually injurious and, as we have just seen, is certainly far removed from that which marked our Lord and Master. It also fails To take account of the need we all have for self-discipline.

A two-fold filling

In both Ephesians and Colossians Paul exhorts us to teach and admonish one another with psalms and hymns and spiritual songs, and in each epistle he first shows us what is the key to doing this. In Ephesians it is, 'Be filled [literally, go on being filled] with the Spirit,' but in Colossians it is, 'Let the word of Christ dwell in you richly.'

God wants us to be 'filled with his Spirit *and* filled with his Word'. It's a cliche but nevertheless true: If it's all Word and no Spirit *we dry* up. If it's all Spirit and no Word we *blow up*. With due attention to both we *grow up!*

God's Word — the acid test

Subjective experience — what goes on inside us — needs constantly to be tested and adjusted by objective truth — the Scriptures.

Church history reveals the wreckage of many a promising revival that began in a true conflagration of the Spirit, but ended in the 'wildfire' of fleshly enthusiasm and satanic deception.

'The Word of God is living and active. Sharper than any double-edged sword, it penetrates even to dividing soul and spirit, joints and marrow; it judges the thoughts and attitudes of the heart.' Only through God's Word may we safely distinguish between what is soulish (of the human soul) and what is spiritual (of the Holy Spirit).

In an issue of faith or practice, what we believe or what we do, our appeal must ever be 'to the law and to the testimony'. You and I will never reach a point here on earth where we shall no longer need the instruction, confirmation and correction of the written Word.

The mark of maturity

God is deeply concerned about our attitude and response to the Scriptures. It grieves him if, after so long a time, we are still babes dependent on spoon-feeding because we cannot feed ourselves, only able to manage milk because we find meat indigestible, needing still to be taught our ABC when we should be able to teach others (Hebrews 5:12-14).

He wants us to live by *every* word that comes from the mouth of God. In other words, the whole book is to be our diet. Though we are not all called to preach, we are all called to exhort one another and build one another up.

Let us take to heart Paul's exhortation to Timothy, 'Present yourself to God as one approved, a workman who does not need to be ashamed and who correctly handles the word of truth' (2 Timothy 2:15).

Prayer warfare

The call of Christ is a call to warfare.

When God informed Moses at the burning bush that he had come down to deliver the Israelites from the land of Egypt to bring them into 'a land flowing with milk and honey', he was careful to add that this was 'the place of the Canaanites, and Hittites, the Amorites . . . ' — in other words, a land occupied by alien powers that would need to be dispossessed.

When at length they came out of Egypt, 'God did not lead them by way of the land of the Philistines, although that was near; for God said, "Lest the people repent when they see war, and return to Egypt." But God led the people round by the way of the wilderness' (Exodus 13:17-18 RSV). They needed desert discipline to prepare them for Canaan conflict.

At Kadesh Barnea, within striking distance of the land, they sent ahead spies who returned with their report that the land was indeed fruitful but that the cities were strongly fortified, and that some of the inhabitants were giants in stature.

The people were filled with alarm. 'Why is the Lord bringing us to this land only to let us fall by the sword?' (Numbers 14:3) they asked. Once again they recoiled in fear at the thought of war. So God had to lead them around until all the old generation had dropped into their wilderness graves and a new generation had arisen who were willing to trust God for the possession of their inheritance.

A charismatic people

In their deliverance from Egypt and passage through the Red Sea Israel had witnessed God's supernatural intervention. This introduced them to a supernatural life in which every day they saw evidences of God's miracle-working power.

Paul reminds the Corinthians of this: 'Our fathers were all under the cloud, and all passed through the sea, and all were baptised into Moses in the cloud and in the sea, and all ate the same supernatural food and all drank the same supernatural drink. For they drank from the supernatural Rock which followed them, and the Rock was Christ' (1 Corinthians 10:1-4 RSV).

In other words, what Paul is saying is that these Israelites were a Spirit-and-water-baptised community. They had all the right experiences. At Marah the bitter waters had been miraculously sweetened. At Meribah the flinty rock had been struck so that the waters gushed out. Every day, as they lifted the tent-flap, bread from heaven lay on the ground.

Their clothes were made of supernatural fibres that never wore out in all those years of their desert wanderings. The pillar of cloud over the tabernacle, unaffected by the desert winds, acted as a sun umbrella and piloted them through the trackless wastes to the next oasis.

Here we come to the punch line in what Paul is saying to the Corinthians. Though they were manifestly charismatic in experience, 'nevertheless with most of them God was not pleased' (v5) and they never took possession of their inheritance. Though they got so far and experienced so much, when it came to God's full purpose they never made it.

This is not simply a solemn lesson for the Corinthians but for us, too: 'These things happened to them as a warning, but they were written down for our instruction, upon whom the end of the ages has come. Therefore let any one who thinks that he stands take heed lest he fall' (v11-12).

Our battles — or his?

Soon after Israel came out of Egypt they were attacked by a nomadic tribe called the Amalekites. It was a fierce one-day battle in which Israel's fortunes ebbed and flowed, but ended in victory.

The decisive factor was not the skill and courage of Joshua and his army down on the plain, but the action of Moses, Aaron and Hur on the hilltop. As Moses, supported by his two companions, held aloft the rod of God, the battle finally turned in Israel's favour.

This teaches us that these 'flesh and blood' Amalekites were not Israel's real enemy. God's people were really up against spiritual forces that were using the Amalekites.

Though there was no question here of fighting to possess any land, God was giving his people a 'dress rehearsal' for the conflict of Canaan. This was the principle by which they would overcome their enemies. As they stood in faith on the mount of God, wielding the rod of God, they would experience the victory of God. He himself would drive out the enemy before them.

After the episode with Amalek, Israel had no further encounter with any other enemy nation throughout their wilderness wanderings till they reached the threshold of the land of Canaan.

In all those intervening years there was plenty of conflict, but it was all *internal*. They battled against the will of God. They fought with their own lusts and desires. They strove to master their own fear and unbelief. Their hands were so full with the internal enemy, they were in no position to engage the enemies of God.

There are believers today, even testifying to the baptism in the Spirit, who still have not entered into their inheritance because they are similarly preoccupied with fighting their own battles and consequently cannot begin to fight the battles of the Lord.

War and rest

It is a deeply instructive paradox that Canaan was not only to be a place of war for Israel, but also a place of rest.

God had said of the earlier generation, 'They shall never enter *my rest*' (Hebrews 3:11). Moses described Canaan in the same way when he said, 'You have not as yet come to *the rest* and to the inheritance which the Lord your God gives you' (Deuteronomy 12:9 RSV). Only those who have entered into rest are able to fight the Lord's battles.

The book of Joshua, with its history of possessing the land, has its New Testament counterpart in Ephesians. It is here that the paradox of rest and war is made plain.

In chapter one we see Christ raised from the dead and made to sit at the Father's right hand in the heavenly places, far above all rule and authority, and with all things placed under his feet. Christ sits because his work of redemption is finished (Hebrews 10:12). He sits because he is resting in the sufficiency of that work. He sits because, as a victorious sovereign, he now exercises the authority of the throne.

This brings us to chapter two. Astonishing though it may seem, the victory of the Head (Christ), though decisive and complete in itself, requires the co-operation of the body (the church) for its full implementation. Note how Paul closes Ephesians 1 by saying that Christ's 'body' is 'the fulness [that is, the completion] of him who fills everything in every way'. Christ is incomplete without his body. It is only in union with his body that there can be a full outworking of his victory on the cross.

That's why we see God's mighty resurrection power working

not only 'in Christ' (1:20) but also in '*you* [when you] were dead in your transgressions and sins' (2:1). And so the amazing plan unfolds. 'God . . . made us alive with Christ . . . raised us up with Christ and seated us with him in the heavenly realms' (2:4-6).

To be seated with Christ means to enter into his rest and to share the authority of his throne. Since he is 'far above all rule and authority', so are we. Since all those powerful spirit forces that control the world are beneath his feet, they are beneath ours, too.

'Seated with Christ' speaks of our position — not a position which we have won, but which has been won for us. When it comes to prayer warfare, *position* is all-important. Instead of fighting *for* it, we fight *from* it, and that makes all the difference.

Aerial warfare

Now we can understand Paul's great classic on spiritual warfare in Ephesians 6.

Before two opposing armies can be locked in combat they must necessarily be in the same place. We have seen where we are — where Christ has put us, 'in the heavenly realms'. This, we are told, is the place where we are at the receiving end for all the resources God has for us (1:3). This is the place where our exalted, victorious Lord is seated at his Father's right hand (1:20). This is where we are seated *with* him and *in* him (2:6).

But chapter six also tells us that this is the sphere of activity of those ruling spirits, 'the principalities and powers' that are arrayed against us, whose powerful commander is described as 'the ruler of the kingdom of the air' (2:2).

Holy Scripture gives us many glimpses of this age-long conflict between God and Satan involving vast angelic forces on both sides. Revelation tells us, 'War arose in heaven, Michael and his angels fighting against the dragon [Satan]; and the dragon and his angels fought, but they were defeated' (12:7-8 RSV).

Sitting or standing?

Ephesians 2 emphasises the believer's *sitting,* but in chapter six we find him *standing.*

If sitting speaks of rest, standing speaks of resistance. All the expressions here speak of defensive warfare. Hence the emphasis on protective armour. Even the sword, an offensive weapon, is essential for resistance. If we have been given a position of victory in Christ we may be sure that Satan will do his devilest, by intimidation or deception, by hook or by crook, to drive us off our vantage ground. 'Stand therefore.'

We are not commanded to attack the devil; we are commanded to resist him. We have only to hold our ground to be in victory.

He will insinuate that only very great saints can attain to such a position. He will whisper that we are not mature enough, not strong enough, not holy enough to occupy this exalted seat. He will strengthen his case by pointing out our weaknesses and failures. This is where we have to resist, equipped with the whole armour of God, especially helmet, breastplate and shield.

Our position is immeasurably strengthened when we also wield 'the sword of the Spirit which is the utterance of God' by coming forth with one of God's utterances, such as 'God says he has raised us up with Christ, and made us sit with him — did you get that, Satan? *God made us sit* with him in the heavenly places.'

The grand objective

Putting on the armour, wielding the sword and withstanding the enemy is all with a grand objective in view: that we may 'pray at all times in the Spirit, with all prayer and supplication' (Ephesians 6:18 RSV).

This is what it means to hold up the rod in the mount of God. This is what it means to exercise the authority of the throne. Prayer in the Spirit means that the Holy Spirit is initiating and motivating, inspiring and energising the prayer. Instead of self-centred praying we have God-centred praying. We begin to receive the Spirit's burdens and objectives. And this is to be 'at all times' — not just occasionally.

My wife and I had an experience of prayer warfare before we really understood anything much about it. Soon after we had set up our first home we saw an announcement about a forthcoming performance in the village hall. The magical feats that this man and his wife claimed to be able to do caused me to say to my wife: 'This thing is either a fraud or satanic; either way I think we should pray against it.'

We did, but with no idea of what would result. The village hall was filled, but at the outset of the programme an argument broke out between the husband and wife. She struck him on the face and the performance broke up in confusion. The audience had their money back and we never heard of the couple again.

The subtle and divisive tactics of Satan are bringing confusion and dissension into many family and church situations. Sometimes these problems continue unresolved year after year.

Counselling and discipline may be in vain. And it is no good trying to cast out demons when they are not in occupation.

The situation calls for us to use the authority of the rod in the mount of God, to pray in the Spirit until we see Satan bruised beneath our feet, to bind the strong man until his goods have been spoiled.

When Israel eventually entered into the conflict of Canaan, they moved in as a body under Joshua. There was a generation that missed it and a generation that experienced it. I believe the greatest victories in the history of the church are still future. They will happen, not because God has raised up great warriors of the calibre of George Müller or John Hyde, but because the body of Christ has risen up to its heavenly privileges and believers are moving in together to take possession of the land.

Behind human rulers are spirit rulers that belong to the kingdom of darkness. Their influence is seen in much of the legislation that finds its way on to the statute books. In many parts of the world they are responsible for whole lands being shut to the gospel.

Authoritative praying can cause bad legislation to be thrown out or, where necessary, repealed. It can cause closed lands to become opened lands. It can shape the destiny of nations.

Is it not time for the saints of the Most High to possess the kingdom, and for men of violence to take it by force?

The radical Christ

God's Holy Spirit is at work to change us into the likeness of Christ. Have we realised what a radical change this means?

In our character studies of Christ we have tended to overlook the revolutionary teacher, the controversialist, the provocative preacher, the implacable opponent of the religious establishment. It is these radical elements in our Lord's character that need to be rediscovered, and then reproduced in the life of every disciple.

A people bored to tears with the platitudes of the scribes and Pharisees gasped in astonishment at the revolutionary teaching that fell from the lips of the prophet of Nazareth. But it wasn't simply his teaching; his lifestyle was wholly in keeping with what he taught. In contrast with the prevailing religious fashion, he focused on people's inward rather than their outward state, on their heart condition, attitude and motive.

His values were diametrically opposed to those of the money-loving Pharisees. With him all material interests were subordinated to the supreme interest of the heavenly kingdom.

His zeal was red hot whenever the honour of his Father was at stake. He burned with indignation when he found tradespeople in his Father's house 'making a mint' at the expense of the worshippers. He kicked over the tables of the moneychangers, scattering their change in all directions, and with a whip of small cords drove them from the sanctuary.

Christ did not hesitate to disregard convention and protocol whenever it stood between him and the will of God, and religious traditions he simply ignored.

In his confrontation with the religious leaders his words and actions were at times intentionally provocative, as though he was determined to bring issues to the surface. He denounced their hypocrisy in the most scathing language. Bad characters and social outcasts, on the other hand, were drawn irresistibly to his circle.

But it was in his handling of people, whether his disciples or others, that his true radicalism was most clearly seen. His discernment and counsel always penetrated with unerring accuracy to the root issue.

Radical family relationships

Whenever we allow the cross of Christ to work in us, biblical radicalism is always the result. For Jesus, the cross was not only an event that lay at the end of his earthly course, but a spiritual principle that characterised every aspect of his life, even his human relationships.

When the wine ran out at the Cana wedding, an acutely embarrassing situation for the hosting family, Mary whispered to her son, 'They have no wine,' with the implied suggestion that he should now use his miraculous power to do something about it.

'O woman, what have you to do with me? My hour has not yet come' (John 2:4 RSV). He had not yet performed his first miracle, and this, as we subsequently learn, was to be the occasion of it. So why the implied rebuke?

Mary had to understand that their relationship had now changed. The timing of this event must be at the prompting of the Spirit. It was at the bidding of his heavenly Father, not of his human mother, that he must now move. Their special relationship had to fade into the background.

This was reinforced when, at a packed house meeting, he was informed that his mother and brothers were outside wanting to see him. That would mean dropping what he was doing.

'Who are my mother and my brothers?' he asked. Then, looking at those seated in a circle around him, he said, 'Here are my mother and my brothers! Whoever does God's will is my brother and sister and mother' (Mark 3:31-35). The claims of the family versus the claims of the ministry was the issue.

This is still the issue on which many a promising ministry has foundered — an unwillingness for the cross to touch family relationships. Jesus summarised the principle in one of the most radical statements he ever uttered: 'If anyone comes to me and does not hate his father and mother, his wife and children, his brothers and sisters — yes, even his own life — he cannot be my disciple' (Luke 14:26).

The divine claims must reign supreme, even in our relationships with our nearest and dearest. Jesus not only taught it, he practised it.

Will it result in injury?

If I am neglecting my family responsibilities 'for the cause of Christ', then I am misapplying what Jesus taught and practised.

Hating father, mother, etc., includes hating one's own life also, and that means embracing the cross. How could the application of the cross to our family relationships ever injure those relationships? The cross may bring hurt, but it will never bring harm. If it doesn't make us better husbands, wives, parents or children, then somehow we've got it wrong.

To be softhearted, sentimental or indulgent towards those we love means that we are more concerned about pleasing them than pleasing God. This, not the other, is the attitude that causes spiritual injury. Though the cross will bring sacrifice and suffering, separation and self-denial, it will always bring blessing.

Applying the principle of 'the cross' to human relationships was the lesson Abraham had to learn, until he was willing in the end to lay Isaac on the altar. And that was the very best thing that Abraham ever did for Isaac — and for himself.

Dealing with the roots

In the handling of men and women Jesus was not only masterly; he was radical. Why didn't he tell the rich young ruler (Luke 18:18-25) to *tithe* his possessions and give that to the poor? Or would it not have been enough to persuade him to imitate the wealthy Zacchaeus and give away *half* of his goods?

No, Jesus told him to sell *all* and give away *all.* Why? His problem was not that he possessed great wealth, but that his great wealth possessed him. The eye of the Surgeon had diagnosed a cancer called 'the love of money', and radical surgery was the only hope.

'Will I have to give up my smoking and drinking?' was the anxious question of a young man seeking salvation.

'Yes, you will,' was the uncompromising answer.

'But giving up smoking and drinking is not a scriptural condition of salvation,' someone will say.

True, but nor is selling all you have and giving to the poor. But when the Holy Spirit pinpoints an issue, *that issue* becomes the battleground on which a person will either yield or resist, receive Christ or reject him. We only hinder the work of the Spirit when we try to shift the fighting from the battlefield that he has chosen to what we consider a more scriptural one. Don't try to be more spiritual than the Holy Spirit. You can never win!

How often Jesus probed his way into the thoughts and intents of a man's heart by means of one carefully chosen question.

'Do you want to get well?' (John 5:6) must have sounded strange to the ears of a chronic invalid. That's what he had been wanting for thirty-eight years. Every day as he lay beside the pool of Bethesda he spent his time hoping against hope that this might be his lucky day.

But had he faced up to all the implications of being healed? To be rid of the pain, weakness and humiliation would be great. But what about being rehabilitated after all those years? What about finding a job, starting to pay his way and support his family, instead of being an object of charity? What about the mending of broken relationships?

Most important of all, what about breaking with the sin that it seems had brough it all upon him? Men and women may want salvation, deliverance, healing or the filling of the Spirit, but if they are unwilling for a change in their way of life there will be no permanent work.

'Sin no more, that nothing worse befall you' were Jesus' last words to this man.

How much do you want it?

Sometimes Jesus treated people in what we might think was an offhand, even discourteous way, but always he had a vital end in view.

There was a royal official who came to plead with Jesus to accompany him to Capernaum and heal his desperately sick son.

'Unless you people see miraculous signs and wonders . . . you will never believe' (John 4:48), was Jesus' seemingly unfeeling response.

'Sir, come down before my child dies,' cried the man in desperation. Only then did Jesus speak the life-giving word, 'You may go. Your son will live.'

Similar were Jesus' tactics with the Canaanite woman whose demonised daughter was suffering grievously (Matthew 15:21-28). At first Jesus did not answer her at all.

'Send her away,' said the disciples, thinking that Jesus didn't want to be bothered with her.

She was further tested when Jesus said, 'I was sent only to the lost sheep of Israel.'

At this the woman knelt before him pleading for help. Surely he will respond now.

'It is not right to take the children's bread and toss it to their dogs,' was his reply.

It is hard to think of anything more provocative for a Jew to say to a Gentile, but it drew from this woman one of the greatest expressions of faith to be found in the gospels: 'Even the dogs eat the crumbs that fall from their masters' table.'

Jesus could withhold no longer. 'Woman, you have great faith! Your request is granted.'

Our Lord's radical approach is urgently needed in the counselling room, when dealing with those seeking salvation or answers for spiritual problems.

There is always the pressure to produce results, to chalk up another success. The counsellor is therefore tempted to make it as easy as possible for people to make the right responses or the right decisions. Jesus, on the other hand, often made it as difficult as possible. He even used parables to veil the truth, 'so that seeing they may *not* see, and hearing they may *not* understand' (Luke 8:10 RSV).

We have to learn from the 'Wonderful Counsellor' that success is not the name of the game. Too many of our 'success' cases prove to be ultimate failures. Jesus himself didn't always achieve success, as men and women define it. There was one point when he suffered a mass defection of disciples. But he always touched the root of the matter and compelled people to face reality.

The radical approach will mean that we shall not always be able to report, 'He came right through.' Sometimes it may have to be, 'He went away sorrowful,' but always there will be the assurance that the word of God has been spoken and the judgment of God has been brought.

Training disciples in faith

If we want to be men and women of faith we must be prepared for the Lord to put us through a rugged training course, for that's how he made the Twelve such stalwarts of faith as we find them to be in the Acts of the Apostles.

Similarly, if we are training others we must subject them to the same kind of radical treatment. Again and again they were 'thrown in the deep end' as he involved them in his own miraculous ministry, such as in the feeding of the four thousand and the five thousand, the walking on the water, the tribute money from the fish's mouth, the two miraculous catches of fish, and of course his sending them forth to drive out evil spirits and heal every kind of sickness and disease.

Many times they had their knuckles rapped when faith did not rise to the occasion.

They were on the Sea of Galilee that they knew so well. 'A furious squall came up, and the waves broke over the boat, so that it was nearly swamped' (Mark 4:37). They had faced storms before, but this was something else. For once these hardened and experienced fishermen took up panic stations, convinced their last moment had come.

It was true that the Lord of all creation was on board, but you wouldn't have thought so by the reactions of these disciples — in the same way that no-one would think that we had him on board when we panic in our own emergencies! So relaxed was Christ that he had fallen asleep despite the storm.

'Lord, save us! We're going to drown!' they cried.

With majestic poise he rose and spoke peace to the raging waters. Then he turned to the trembling disciples. Surely they needed calming, comforting and reassuring. But listen to his words: 'You of little faith, why are you afraid?'

No excuses allowed

When Jesus came down from the Mount of Transfiguration he found a demonised boy, a shamefaced bunch of disciples and a gesticulating father trying to explain that these followers of his had failed to heal his son (Matthew 17:14-18). Up till now they had achieved great success in dealing with evil spirits, so that this must have been a humiliating experience for them.

'I'm sorry you didn't succeed with this difficult case, but you did your best' was *not* how he responded to their failure. He issued a rebuke before that watching, listening crowd that must have made those disciples feel about the size of Tom Thumb!

'O unbelieving and perverse generation,' he said, 'how long shall I stay with you? How long shall I put up with you? Bring the boy here to me.' And then to crown their humiliation he drove out the demon with a word.

Similar was the occasion when Peter, responding to the word of Jesus, began to imitate his Master by walking on the water (Matthew 14:25-33). Remember, the disciples had not yet received the Holy Spirit. They were not yet fully moving in the supernatural as they were to do after Pentecost. Yet here was Peter doing what no-one other than Christ had ever done.

Then came the attack of fear, the 'sinking feeling' and the cry for help to which Jesus instantly responded: 'Never mind, Peter, you did actually walk on the water. Well done! Those other disciples didn't dare.'

No. Peter didn't get off so lightly. 'You of little faith,' said Jesus. 'Why did you doubt?'

Unbelief is always blameworthy

When Jesus met with his disciples in resurrection we learn that 'he *rebuked* them for their lack of faith and their stubborn refusal to believe those who had seen him after he had risen' (Mark 16:14). He had frequently forewarned his disciples of his impending death, and given them the promise of his rising again. Their failure to believe was therefore inexcusable, and his rebuke correspondingly severe.

If it seems to us that at times Jesus was a little hard on his disciples we have only to look ahead into the Acts to see what men of faith they became.

In *The Fourth Dimension,* Paul Yonggi Cho of Korea shares with the reader how he became a man of faith. God does not seem to have made the training course in faith any easier for twentieth century saints. We need to be tough with ourselves, and if we have responsibility for training others, we must be tough with them, if ever we are to see a generation arise who will really believe God.

Conformist or non-conformist?

Here we must leave uncompleted our pen portrait of the radical Christ. For the moment let us notice that every aspect of Christ's radicalism is in perfect accord with all that we know of the ways and character of God. In his radicalism, as in everything else, Jesus was 'the express image' of his heavenly Father.

Face to face with the radical Christ we have to ask ourselves whether we are yet 'conformed to the likeness of [God's] Son' (Romans 8:29).

If not, let us bring to God those specific areas in which we know ourselves to be lacking, and ask him to work those in us by his Spirit, and so reproduce in us the likeness of Jesus. He wants to make us just as radical as his Son in every area of our lives.

A root out of dry ground

Laid at birth in a cattle-trough. Reared in a working-class home. Apprenticed at the carpenter's bench. Developing his spiritual life amidst the sterile religion of Judaism. This was the unpromising background of Jesus of Nazareth, Messiah of Israel and Saviour of the world.

In what is perhaps the most sublime prediction of his sufferings and glory to be found in the writings of the prophets, Isaiah describes him as growing up before his Father 'like a tender shoot, and like *a root out of dry ground*' (Isaiah 53:2). It did not please the heavenly Husbandman to shelter that 'tender shoot' by supernatural power from the grim realities of 'those crude and cruel days, when human flesh was cheap'.

Here certainly was a root out of dry ground. He displayed life and fruitfulness when all around him was death and barrenness. The spiritual freshness that he brought contrasted with the stale religious atmosphere that hung over the land. In a word, he was *the contradiction of his environment.*

This involved him in a protest movement. In fact, the Founder of the Christian faith was himself the first true protestant. He declared, 'The world . . . hates me because I testify that what it does is evil.'

'Whoever claims to live in him must walk as Jesus did' (1 John 2:6). When he prayed for his followers he did not ask the Father to take them out of the world, but to protect them in the world (John 17:15). What then was the danger?

It was twofold. First that, living in a secular world, they themselves would become secularised. In other words, that the world would invade the church. For the ship to be in the sea is normal, but when the sea gets into the ship it can be fatal. What the devil failed to achieve in the first century by persecution he later effected by patronisation. Christ has called us to be the salt of the earth, because the earth is corrupt, and to be the light of the world, because the world is dark.

The second danger is that, while still living in the world, we try to escape from it by retreating into our spiritual ghettoes. This is defeatism. It implies that God cannot preserve us in this evil age. What was intended to be a tender plant supernaturally preserved in the midst of a hostile environment then becomes a hothouse plant that can never reproduce itself in the earth.

To fulfil our function as salt we have to permeate society. Whoever preserved a barrel of fish by putting fish in one barrel and salt in another?

Jesus said that the kingdom of God had come upon people. He was announcing an invasion from heaven. We are part of it. Let us go forth to 'fill the earth with the sound of his praise'.

The hidden springs

'A prophet of God' — what does the phrase conjure up in your mind? Moses stretching out his rod to part the Red Sea? Elijah calling down fire from heaven? Or maybe Agabus predicting a severe famine throughout the world?

I am not so concerned here with the spectacular revelations or demonstrations of the prophet as with the hidden springs of his life and ministry. Or to put it more colloquially, let's find out what makes the prophet tick.

According to God's estimate, *being* takes precedence over *doing*. In other words, God's primary concern is with a man's character, and only secondarily with his ministry. The reason for this is not far to seek. What we *do* must spring from what we *are*, and if what we do appears more spiritual than what we are, sooner or later (and it is usually sooner) our doing is sabotaged.

This is vividly illustrated by the tragic history of Samson, whose spectacular feats against the Philistines were offset by his own carnality. In the end he spent his last days a prisoner of his enemies, and never achieved a full deliverance for Israel.

All the basic principles that govern the New Testament prophetic ministry are to be found in Old Testament teaching, especially when we investigate the hidden springs. Let us look at the earliest prophets mentioned in the Bible.

We have to reach almost the closing book of the Bible before we learn that the first prophet in the history of humankind was *Enoch*. We would never have known if Jude had not told us (Jude 14). We don't usually think of Enoch as a prophet but as the saintly man who walked with God for three hundred years. Just to think that we consider ourselves to have really accomplished something if we have a day's unbroken fellowship with God!

So Enoch, living as he did at the dawn of human history, set the standard for all successive generations of prophets. Someone has described him as an Alpine climber last seen heading for the summit. And of course we have the inside story. He didn't slip and break his neck. He made it.

The prophet is called first and foremost to a life of intimacy with God. It wasn't that Enoch had it in him. It wasn't that he was made that way. The record in Genesis 5 makes it clear that he didn't start to walk with God till he reached what we now regard as retiring age. Life really began for Enoch at sixty-five! That should teach us that it's never too late.

The friend of God

This brings us to Abraham. He is the first man that God ever called a prophet, and in quite a surprising connection. Not because he brought some stupendous prediction like Enoch, who prophesied the day of the Lord at the dawn of human history. A tribal king called Abimelech had taken Abraham's wife for his harem, thinking her to be Abraham's sister, with the result that a judgment of barrenness had fallen on his household. God spoke to him in a dream, and having explained the situation told him: 'Now return the man's wife, for *he is a prophet, and he will pray for you* and you will live' (Genesis 20:7).

So the first thing God ever said about a prophet was that he was a man with access to God — not just a man who prayed, but a man who got his prayers answered!

It is significant that Abraham the prophet was also called 'God's friend' (2 Chronicles 20:7; James 2:23), and this is clearly illustrated in connection with his prayer life. God was about to bring destruction on the cities of Sodom and Gomorrah for their heinous wickedness.

'Shall I hide from Abraham what I am about to do?' God asked himself.

Why would he ask such a question? Because Abraham was his friend, with whom he was accustomed to sharing his secrets, so he shared this one with him. The result was what God intended. Abraham got involved. He wrestled with God in prayer. Although these two great cities were not saved by Abraham's praying, Lot and his family were, and that would have been one of Abraham's major concerns in his intercession.

This friendship, this intimacy with God, is one of the most beautiful features of Abraham's life. God loved to walk with him under the stars and share with him his heavenly secrets. Sometimes the magnitude of what God promised him was enough to stagger his faith, but 'Abraham staggered not'.

'Look up in the night sky, my friend,' God would say to him when he still had no child, 'and try to count the stars. That's how numerous your descendants will be.' And on another occasion, 'Look as far as you can to the north, to the south, to the east and to the west. All this land I am going to give to your descendants.'

So the prophet is privileged to share God's secrets and to know what God plans to do. 'Surely the Lord God does nothing, without revealing his secret to his servants the prophets' (Amos 3:7 RSV).

The man of God

The next great prophet in the line of succession was *Moses*.

We may think of him as the prophet *par excellence* of the Old Testament for he enjoyed face-to-face communion with God beyond that generally experienced by prophets. God said, 'I reveal myself to [a prophet] in visions, I speak to him in dreams. But this is not true of my servant Moses . . . . With him I speak face to face, clearly and not in riddles' (Numbers 12:6-8).

To him it was revealed that the greatest prophet of all, the coming Messiah, would be a prophet like himself (Deuteronomy 18:15). Moses' uniqueness is confirmed by his obituary: 'Since then, no prophet has arisen in Israel like Moses, whom the Lord knew face to face' (Deuteronomy 34:10).

There are two expressions used of Moses that are characteristic, and that must shape our whole thinking about the hidden springs of the prophet's ministry. The first we find in the above quotation from Numbers, when God refers to him as 'my servant Moses'. Again and again he is called 'the servant of the Lord'.

In coming to know God, the prophet's attitudes and inner disposition have been so shaped that all self-possession, self-importance and independence of spirit have been eliminated. His posture before the Lord is that of the servant waiting at the doorpost to come at the master's call or to run to do his bidding or to stand forth to speak his word.

The other expression is 'Moses, the man of God'. From then on 'man of God' became a synonym for a prophet. It is used of Samuel and of David, of Elijah and of Elisha. Many prophets in the record are anonymous. We simply read, 'A man of God came.' What does the expression suggest? That here is someone whose relationship with God is deep and intimate and real. He knows God.

Has anything brushed off?

A brother and I were discussing a young man in the church whose lack of spiritual progress was giving us cause for concern, when my friend remarked, 'What he needs is a big dose of God.' The same could be said of many believers.

A prophet is someone who has had just that. That is what we must have if we are to be a prophetic people. There must be a God-consciousness about us. We must feel at home in his presence. Our fellowship with God must be one of reverent intimacy. Something of the inner life of the man of God must characterise the inner life of the people of God.

Inevitably a man of God is someone in whom a goodly measure of the character of God has been formed. There is a saying, 'You can't walk with God, spend time with God, without something of God brushing off.' There were many sons of the prophets in the time of Elisha, but the woman of Shunem discerned there was something different about Elisha. She described him as 'a holy man of God'.

When Elijah suddenly appeared in the court of King Ahab with an ultimatum from heaven, no-one knew who he was or where he came from. So first he presented his credentials: 'As the Lord the God of Israel lives, *before whom I stand . . .*' (1 Kings 17:1 RSV).

Here was an ambassador who had come from heaven's court, who was accustomed to standing before the King of kings. These are the only true credentials of a New Testament prophet. He is a man who stands before God. He comes to men and women from God's presence to speak God's word. This is the secret of his authority.

There are those today, even as in the past, who claim to be prophets, but who cannot produce these credentials. They have not been standing before God. They have not been hearing what God was saying. They speak the visions of their own minds, the thoughts of their own hearts, and not from the mouth of the Lord. They may even speak what is true and biblical, but it is not God's 'now' word.

Listen to what God says about such: 'I did not send these prophets, yet they have run with their message; I did not speak to them, yet they have prophesied. But *if they had stood in my council,* they would have proclaimed my words to my people' (Jeremiah 23:21-22).

Say not, 'For prophets only'

There is always a temptation to put prophets, whether biblical ones or present-day ones, on a spiritual pedestal. 'They must be made of different stuff from us,' we say to ourselves.

James will not allow us to get away with such thinking. He tells us first that we must look on them as examples to follow, especially in their patient suffering (James 5:10). Then, in holding up Elijah before us as an example of a man who prevailed in prayer, he anticipates our objections by saying that he was 'a man just like us' (5:17). At one point Elijah ran away in fear, and then even gave way to self-pity and self-justification. Nevertheless he accomplished the will of God.

Let me say it again: the prophets are our examples. They are there to challenge and inspire us. We are to be motivated by the same prophetic spirit. How could it be otherwise if we are indeed a prophetic people?

Prophets were never intended to monopolise the audience chamber of the King of kings, or to 'corner' fellowship with God. There are many councils over which the Almighty presides, and if you are not called to stand before God in the same council as the prophet, be assured that there is one in which your name is called, and where God will share secrets that you need to hear.

The health of that houseplant in your home is determined in great measure by what lies below the surface of the soil. You cannot have a healthy plant and an unhealthy root. Let me ask you: What have you got beneath the surface? Is the hidden life robust and strong, or weak and sickly? Is your spiritual root system suffering from neglect? What about the hidden springs? Have they dried up?

It is in this hidden area that the life of the prophet should provoke and challenge us.

How do we get there?

Once we are convinced that such a life of fellowship with God is for us, too, the big question is how to get there.

'You will seek me and find me,' God is still saying, 'when you search for me *with all your heart.*' Those who experience it are those who want it badly. There are scores of true believers who would love it, yet they never enjoy it. Why? Because they don't want it with all their heart. Those who enter in are those who hunger and thirst for it.

This is invariably where the failure lies. The remedy is to ask God to show us why we are not hungry for him. It may be for the same reasons that the seed of the sower did not bring forth fruit (Luke 8:11-14). If so, when we have dealt with all that he has shown us, we will find a growing hunger within.

Otherwise it may be simply lack of motivation. We must ask

God to show us the unspeakable honour and privilege of being invited to stand before the God of the whole earth. 'Blessed is the man you choose and bring near to live in your courts!' What joy! What fulfilment! What fruitfulness! What harmony! What security!

Once we are really motivated there must come the discipline of curtailment. Some of us will never find God in this way because we are much too busy working for him. Our activism is our biggest hindrance. We must lay aside all our self-justifying arguments and learn all over again from the story of Mary and Martha what our Lord and Master considers is 'the one thing needful'.

Also, we must learn to wait on God by restraining our much speaking in his presence. Only so can we train our ears to listen. There are some fifteen or more Hebrew words used in the Old Testament that are translated 'wait', but with various shades of meaning such as to wait patiently, to wait in silence, to wait expectantly, to wait in hope and to wait earnestly.

If we are constant and persevering, God will draw near and speak. He will reveal himself to us, and we shall understand what it was that so captivated King David that this fellowship with God, despite all the affairs of state, became his consuming passion:

'One thing I ask of the Lord, this is what I seek; that I may dwell in the house of the Lord all the days of my life, to gaze upon the beauty of the Lord and to seek him in his temple' (Psalm 27:4).

Lost your cutting edge?

The logger was helping to construct a new community centre by the river, and was swinging a borrowed axe when the head flew off.

What's the good of swinging an axe-handle with no axe-head? About as good as pushing a lawnmower with no blades! However, the prophet was on hand to bring him a word of wisdom (2 Kings 6:1-7). Some of us Christians are in the same situation — and this is a word for us.

Entrusted ministry

I was far away from home and the couple I was staying with had been very kind; helping in the garden was the least I could do. The garden tools, however, were a bit rickety — at least, that's my story.

First, I broke the rake. After that, an old fork. Finally, it was the rusty old shears — 'Just came apart in my hands, brother.' They were a truly sanctified couple and didn't actually say, 'You ham-fisted old so-and-so!' But looks can do the job equally well.

You feel terrible when you break or lose what doesn't belong to you. Had it been his own axe, the logger would probably have just written it off, but his deep concern was that it was borrowed. He felt accountable.

The axe you hold in your hand is not your own. The Master Builder entrusted it to you when he called you to do that job. None of us *own* our ministry. Paul viewed himself as a steward, 'entrusted with the gospel' (1 Thessalonians 2:4). Jesus often emphasised this, as in the parables of the unjust steward, the talents and the pounds.

We can't afford to become possessive or protective of our ministry, because it's not ours at all — it's his. And at the end of the day the Boss will examine our work and we will hand in our tools.

Ineffective

When you lose your axe-head you lose your cutting edge.

You can carry on, going through the motions, swinging the axe-handle — and accomplishing nothing. You can use the right jargon, even do all the right things, but your ministry is ineffective. You become a teacher who imparts truth but doesn't edify the body; an evangelist who preaches fine messages but people aren't saved; a counsellor who is always counselling but never resolving problems; an intercessor who is always praying but never getting answers.

Of course, you could be doing what God *hasn't* appointed, but if your ministry is truly God-given, there's only one conclusion: you must have lost your axe-head.

Competent ministers

My boyhood home in Ireland was by the River Liffey. Many a happy hour I spent with a home-made rod and line, 'casting' just like the experts on the opposite bank, but I never remember catching any fish!

In ministry we can go through the motions for a long time, pass muster with our colleagues and yet hardly be aware that our ministry is ineffective.

It was Paul's testimony that God 'has made us *competent* as ministers of a new covenant' (2 Corinthians 3:6). Competence in God's service is not an optional extra — it's in the job description!

Another way Scripture puts it is, 'bearing fruit in every good work' (Colossians 1:10). The measure of lasting fruit in my service for him is the measure of my effectiveness.

Recovery

'Where did it fall?' was Elisha's vital question.

You want to recover your axe-head? You'll find it just where you lost it. Some of you may know it has gone, yet you don't know where or why. But God does. Enquire of him, and keep on enquiring until you find out.

Here are some places where you will often find lost axe-heads:

☐ Where you allowed bitterness and unforgiveness to seep into your relationships

☐ Where your motives were corrupted by pride, greed or competitiveness

☐ Where you got angry with God because of what he allowed — or didn't allow

☐ Where your dedication was defiled by a worldly spirit

But whatever caused the loss of that cutting edge, you need to get it back. The culprit is always the flesh (or sinful nature) that is continually in conflict with the Spirit (Galatians 5:17-21).

It is the flesh that robs us of our cutting edge. And what is God's answer to the flesh? Here the spiritual lesson in the story is crystal clear. The river where the axe-head sank without trace was the Jordan. Is that significant? The axe-head went down into the water and then came up out of the water. Does that say anything?

Embracing the cross

You may have been baptised — but has *your ministry?*

It is only the cross that can deal with all that robs our ministry of its cutting edge. The cross isn't something we meet at the outset of our Christian life, then leave behind as we press on for our share of the goodies. We take it with us (Luke 14:27).

Do we want our ministry marked by resurrection life? That means taking the way of the cross. The grain of wheat has to die for the harvest to come (John 12:24). Death has to work in us that life may work in others (2 Corinthians 4:12).

If you have known the Spirit's power but have lost your cutting edge, stop praying for a fresh anointing. Embrace the cross in your ministry so that the Spirit who is still resting upon you may be released to flow through you, making you more effective for God than you have ever been before.

Church in perspective

A church is radical in the measure in which it is composed of radical people, that is, people who take a radical rather than a *laissez-faire* attitude to what God has to say about his church.

Many Christians seem to have a blind spot here. They can be radical in their approach to Christian behaviour, to personal discipleship, to the work of the Holy Spirit, to evangelism, to ministry or to Christian responsibility in social issues, but non-radical when it comes to the controversial matter of church.

Here our spiritual understanding and judgment are so easily clouded by custom or tradition, by a misplaced sense of loyalty to our religious roots, by sentimental attachment to the past.

All who have broken new ground for God down the centuries have had to break through these influences. Today, no-one thinks it radical to preach the gospel in the open air, but when Whitefield began to do this it was viewed as highly irregular. Even Wesley, who followed him in the practice, acknowledged how strange it was to him: 'Having been all my life so tenacious of every point relating to decency and order I should have thought the saving of souls almost a sin if it had not been done in a church.'

Some take the view that 'form' and 'structure' are of minor importance. What we need is 'the power'. If that was what was needed the current move of the Spirit would surely have had a far greater impact on the outside community than it has.

People have said, 'Let's not argue about church matters, but get on with the business of living the Christian life and saving souls.' But that is like the woodsman who is too busy felling trees to stop and sharpen his blunt axe. What he needs is not more power, but a sharper tool to make effective use of the power he's got.

Since godly and spiritual people differ so fundamentally in their convictions about the church, many have questioned whether Scripture provides us with a clear word on the issue. Is A. Alexander right when he says, 'God often leaves his servants to find out by experience what is most expedient'? Is it a question of human judgment in the light of changing circumstances?

The history of God's house in Scripture gives us a clear and unequivocal answer to these questions. When God wanted his people to build him a house, he showed Moses a scale model and told him, 'I want it just like that.' Nothing was left to personal judgment, least of all to personal whim and fancy. Every pin and socket was to be made 'according to the pattern'.

It was the same with Solomon's temple. David gave his son the plans 'that the Spirit had put in his mind'. It was all in writing by 'the hand of the Lord'.

If God was so meticulous under the old covenant, can we imagine him being any less under the new? We, too, have it all in writing by the hand of the Lord in the New Testament, but to interpret the teaching aright we must understand the change that has been effected by the introduction of the new covenant.

In the Old Testament God had a sanctuary for his people; in the New God has his people for a sanctuary.

In the Old Testament there was a material house; in the New there is a spiritual house.

In the Old Testament there was a divine pattern; in the New there are divine principles.

With the one there is a fixed form; with the other there is a flexible body.

When people impose on the congregation a rigid and uniform structure, whether of the traditional and historic variety, or based on the misconception that there is in the New Testament an inflexible pattern for church life, they are going back 'under law'. There was undoubtedly great variety in the New Testament churches, but with all the diversity there was also a striking similarity, because they all operated according to the same divine principles. The challenge of the New Testament is to embrace principles, not forms.

Imagine the feeling of a couple who, having allowed some friends to make use of their home, return to find that the furnishings have been drastically altered. The piano in the lounge has been moved to the other side of the room. Valuable oil paintings have been taken down and stored in the attic, and the lovely curtains in the dining-room have been replaced by some others with a ghastly design. It all sounds preposterous, but that is, in effect, what Christendom has done with God's house over the centuries.

So slowly were the changes effected, invariably in times of spiritual decline, that people were hardly aware of what was happening.

God's ways for his church will only function when God's power is at work. With the decline of true godliness the Holy Spirit gradually withdrew. Instead of rectifying the evil, and thus securing the Spirit's return, men and women looked round for human expedients, ways of keeping the wheels turning apart from the Spirit. That necessitated introducing human machinery that God had never envisaged. Things were thrown out that should have been kept in, and things were brought in that should have been kept out.

Ahaz was a very religious king who brought a lot of new religious ideas into God's house. He removed the altar of burnt offering (a type of 'the cross') from its central position in the outer court of the temple, and made it a bloodless vehicle for seeking God's guidance. In its place he introduced a heathen altar that had caught his fancy in Damascus.

All in the space of two incredible verses we read, 'King Ahaz took away . . . and removed . . . . He removed . . . . He took away . . . and removed' (2 Kings 16:17-18).

This has been repeated in church history. Every removal spells loss, and every loss needs to be recovered, for nothing God has ordained for his house is superfluous.

The revivals under Hezekiah and Josiah were times of *removal* as well as of recovery — but the removal, this time, of every unclean thing from the temple. Everything in God's house introduced by men and women which contradicts or renders ineffective the principles that God has established, is unclean. They may be hoary with antiquity, but their age does not make them any more acceptable to God. They may be the product of yesterday, but their novelty does not impress God either.

It takes radical people, undeterred by tradition, sentiment or personal preference, to throw out what does not belong and to restore everything that does. Nothing less will produce a radical New Testament church.

Why community?

Community is not another 'thing' recovered by the charismatic movement. It is of the very essence of the church, and the very lifestyle of the kingdom.

The church is community. We have only to encourage the church to be what it is in order to achieve maximum fruitfulness and effectiveness. But what do we mean by community?

The word is closely associated with 'communion' or 'fellowship'. It describes a company of people who are committed to 'the shared life', in contrast with those whose way of life is individualistic. The crow and the rook, though alike in many respects, have this outstanding difference: the crow is a loner — invariably he is by himself or with his mate — while the rook is gregarious, that is, 'given to association with others of the same species'.

God designed his people to be gregarious, and for a number of very important reasons.

Commune or community?

Nowadays one has only to mention the magic word 'community' in certain circles to conjure up the associated ideas of community of goods, a common purse, two or more families living under the same roof.

In the beginnings of the early church we read that those who believed 'had all things in common' and 'no-one said that any of the things which he possessed was his own' (Acts 2:44; 4:32 RSV). These passages are invariably cited in support of communal living.

The principle of New Testament giving is not that 'others should be eased and you burdened, but that . . . your abundance at the present time should supply their want' (2 Corinthians 8:14 RSV). So the houses and property that those first believers sold were surplus to requirements.

We are not told that they sold up their homes to buy larger ones and live together. We do not find any mention in the Acts of this sort of communal living. Nor did the community of goods which they practised mean that they did not *possess* anything. Acts 4:32 says, 'No-one *claimed* that any of his *possessions* was his own.' It means that they did not hold what they possessed to themselves, but gladly released what they had to meet the needs of others.

I am not saying that communal living is wrong. It is only wrong to make it the norm. To do so may be a substitute for bringing *the whole body* into community.

All believers are called to community living, but certainly not all are called to communal living. Many teenagers in our churches are minors, living at home under the authority of unbelieving parents. Many members are adults with unconverted partners. What prospect have they of selling up and moving into communal living, or turning their homes into extended households? They must not be made to feel that they are second class citizens, or that they are debarred from experiencing community, in the full sense of that term.

There is no better illustration of what is meant by community than the human body. Its many organs, though of great diversity, share a common life and a common purpose, and work harmoniously together. 'The body' was, in fact, Paul's favourite way of describing the church community.

My particular concern here is the basic question of why God designed the church this way. Why are togetherness and interdependence the warp and woof of our spiritual existence?

Answers to wrong attitudes

God designed that faith, not works, should be the door to salvation, because that cuts man down to size, levels his pride to the dust and prepares him to receive salvation as a gift.

In the same way, community lays an axe to the root of man's tendency to self-sufficiency and independence. So long as these attitudes are maintained, a breakdown in community is inevitable. It is a strange thing that in salvation a person may express his great need of God, and yet thereafter maintain an attitude of independence towards his brother. Paul put his finger on this when he said, 'The eye cannot say to the hand, "I have no need of you."'

Whatever lies behind the strong independent spirit that characterises many otherwise spiritual people — whether it is rooted in pride, fear of being exposed or hurt, or some other form of insecurity — it needs to be seen for what it is. It is not the inevitable expression of a strong personality, but a sin against 'the body' and therefore a sin against Christ.

This wrong attitude lies behind the failure of many believers to commit themselves to any local expression of the body of Christ. They like to keep their options open. They don't want to get too close or too involved with anyone. They prefer friendly links that don't cramp their style or limit their freedom.

Such people are themselves the losers, as well as robbing their brothers and sisters, because not only does community cry out, 'You need your brother,' but also 'Your brother needs you.' My independence deprives my brother of the blessing and encouragement of ministering to me and contributing to my spiritual development. It means also that I am depriving him of what God has given me to contribute to his upbuilding.

Individualism is a form of selfishness, while the wheels of community are turned by the mainspring of love. Sharing and caring go together. If love for one another is to be more than mere sentiment, it must be expressed in the context of a deep commitment to one's fellow-Christians — what Paul describes as being 'knitted and joined'.

Drawing the unbeliever

In the beautiful description given us in Acts 2 of the lifestyle of the primitive church we read, 'Attending the temple together and breaking bread in their homes, they partook of food with glad and generous hearts, praising God and having favour with all the people. And the Lord added to their number day by day those who were being saved.'

Here was community in action, and it gave them 'favour with all the people'. What a contrast to the spirit of the world — 'Every man for himself, and devil take the hindermost.' No wonder it was so appealing and attractive to the outside world.

Clearly, it was not so much through organised evangelistic activity as through the practical expression of the love of God by means of community that drew the people to Christ. This has well been called 'the spontaneous expansion of the church'. Certainly there was powerful preaching and widespread witnessing on the part of the rank and file believers, but behind it all was the irrefutable argument of a people who did not simply profess to love each other, but who demonstrated it in a thousand practical ways that the world could see.

In a world saturated with propaganda, something more is needed than zealous gospel preaching. People caught up in the rat race, ever straining for a higher and higher standard of living, and becoming increasingly dissatisfied and disillusioned in the process, want a gospel that can be seen as well as heard.

As with many churches nowadays who give practical expression to community, we seek to help each other with such jobs as gardening, decorating and household repairs. When one of our number is moving house, a van is hired, and then the church muscle in and do the removal.

When we were moved this way to our present home, the couple next door, who had made it clear that they hadn't much time for 'church' in the accepted sense, were clearly impressed.

'Is that the kind of thing you do in your church?' asked the wife. 'That's surely what church ought to be like. How do you join?'

That gave us the opportunity to share Jesus with her.

Maturing the believer

The object of God in all his dealings with us is to bring us to maturity.

The interaction between ourselves and our fellow-believers is an indispensable element in the maturing process. Loners and individualists will always remain underdeveloped in certain areas of their lives, because they are short-circuiting the divine purpose.

Essential to that maturing is a work of purifying that is not accomplished by sitting together in church. It means being thrown together in life situations. Most of us can be reasonably spiritual on our own. It is alongside someone else that attitudes and reactions begin to surface, and the sparks begin to fly.

To dwell above with saints we love,
That surely will be glory;
To dwell below with saints we know,
That's quite a different story!

Learning how to 'dwell below' is the only way we shall be fitted to 'dwell above'.

'But you don't know that brother I have to work with. He seems to bring out the worst in me.'

Well, I suppose that's the reason God put you alongside him!

It's a sobering thought that my brother's or sister's unspirituality never *created* any unspirituality in me. It only caused my own to surface. Nothing can come out except what is already in! The person who shrinks back from the close commitment of community living is escaping from one of God's most effective crucibles, in which God purifies his believer-priests that they might present right offerings to him.

To be subjected to the fire, to become molten till the dross of our unspirituality lies exposed for all to see, is an unpleasant experience. To suffer the skimming away of that dross is a messy business. But, oh, the joy when we are determined to go through with God — which means of course, determined to go through with our brothers and sisters!

'When he has tried me,' cried Job, 'I shall come forth as gold' — and a very big element in that trial was bearing with those three 'friends' who came supposedly to comfort him, but in reality to condemn him. Job only got through when he was willing to pray for them.

God has also designed community to facilitate our maturing by providing the security in which we may grow and develop. Having lots of people around us is no remedy for loneliness. Our teeming cities are full of lonely people. You can attend a packed church and be lonely. The answer is not in people, but in a *relationship* with people, and that's what community is all about.

What a difference it makes to feel loved and protected, and to know that you have significance and worth in the eyes of your fellow-Christians.

An essential element in our maturing is the stimulation afforded by a close relationship with others who are pressing on with God.

This is particularly true in relationship to our ministry in the body of Christ. We are not stimulated by those with whom we only have a nodding acquaintance, or with whom we merely shake hands and exchange a few words of greeting once a week after church. It comes through a committed relationship.

We act and react as iron sharpens iron. That brother's freedom in worship releases me. His zeal in witnessing stimulates me to do the same. That sister's effective intercession quickens my prayer life. The prophesying of one will trigger off the prophesying of others. So our gifts are developed and we reach out for more that others have entered into.

There is a discipline in community life, and we must not run from it if we really want to reach spiritual maturity. It is the discipline of giving and forgiving, bearing and forbearing, of submitting to the authority of those who love us enough to tell us when we are wrong.

To abandon our independence and submit to community is

to leave a world of make-believe and touch down in a world of spiritual reality. If you think you have 'arrived', someone is sure to enlighten you. If you don't quite know where you are, you'll find someone around who does. But be assured of this, you need your brothers and sisters to challenge you, stimulate you and envision you. It is not on our own, but 'with all the saints' that we comprehend 'what is the breadth and length and height and depth of the love of Christ'.

Release of power

Satan has good ground for fearing a company of Christians who have discovered community. He knows that they present a greater threat to his kingdom than any mighty miracle ministry of a spiritual loner. That is why he will do all in his power to discourage, oppose or divide such a company who are really getting it together.

Jesus referred to this power of acting in unison in relation to prayer when he said, 'If two of you agree on earth about anything they ask, it will be done for them by my Father in heaven.' Jesus was not speaking of mere mental agreement, or consenting to pray for the same thing, but an agreement effected by the Spirit in the hearts of those who are seeking him. As the church moves into community living we may expect to see spectacular answers to prayer as this condition is fulfilled and the promise claimed.

We have already seen that the secret of the mighty impact of the early church on the world of their day was not through star performers, such as Peter or Paul, but through the community living of ordinary believers.

Even Peter's great sermon on the day of Pentecost is not presented as a solo performance, for we read, 'Peter, standing with the eleven, lifted up his voice.' And Paul's great missionary journeys were always a team effort carried through with the full support and involvement of the base church at Antioch. It is out of community that the church will finally fulfil her evangelistic mission.

Some years ago a fellow-minister and I were discussing why it was that certain spiritual gifts were being manifested in the move of the Holy Spirit, but very little in the way of signs and wonders. As we bowed together in prayer God told us in prophecy that he would indeed manifest his power in this way, but through his body coming into maturity. The latter-day manifestation of his power would not be through big men, but through the corporate functioning of his body.

Praise be to God, we are much nearer to that than when he spoke those words to us several years ago. It will surely happen, so let's be wholly involved and deeply committed in the community where we know God has planted us.

This business of judging

'Joe Bloggs is a really sincere brother. I'm sure he means well, *but* . . . .'

'Sue Snooks is basically a lovely sister — heart of gold, do anything for you, *but* . . . .'

So many believers seem to suffer from an abnormal development of the critical faculty. I doubt if there is anything more devastating to interpersonal relationships than a critical spirit.

This is how poison spreads in the body of Christ, from tongue to ear. Thomas Watson, the Puritan divine, used to say that he who maligned his brother had the devil in his tongue, and he who listened to him had the devil in his ear!

Judgment is a wonderful faculty that man possesses, enabling him to weigh, to discern, to reach sound opinions and wise decisions. It is in constant operation, from the trivial and almost unconscious decision to wear this particular shirt or put on that dress today, to a crucial business decision that may spell success or disaster for the firm. As believers, it touches every area of our lives and, like every other faculty, needs to be firmly placed under the sway of the Spirit of God.

The use of this faculty

From the outset of the Christian life we have to learn to distinguish right from wrong and truth from error.

God referred to young children who have not come to the age of accountability as those 'who cannot tell their right hand from their left' (Jonah 4:11). Similarly it is spiritual babes who find it difficult to distinguish right from wrong, while 'the mature . . . have their faculties trained by practice to distinguish good from evil' (Hebrews 5:14 RSV). The right development of our judgment is a very important aspect of our growth into maturity.

'The meek will he guide in judgment' (Psalm 25:9 KJV) means that the submissive are guided by means of their own judgment. It is not by dreams, visions or prophecies that God normally guides, nor was it in Bible times, but by a sanctified judgment under the influence of the Holy Spirit.

Concerning the unmarried, Paul says, 'I have no commandment of the Lord [i.e. no direct revelation]: yet I give my judgment' (1 Corinthians 7:25 KJV). Since his judgment is recorded in the sacred writings it is just as much inspired as if he had received a direct revelation. So for us to be guided by the Lord through our judgment is just as valid and spiritual as receiving a special word from him.

The one and only time Jesus spoke of 'the church' as a local congregation was in the context of interpersonal relationships: 'If your brother sins against you' (Matthew 18:15). The first step is to see that brother alone. Then to take along one or two others. Finally, it has to come before the church, and if the brother is still unrepentant the church must pass judgment: 'Treat him as a pagan or a tax collector.'

Paul rebukes the Corinthians for going to law against fellow-believers 'before the ungodly . . . instead of before the saints' (1 Corinthians 6:1). 'Do you not know that the saints will judge the world? And if you are to judge the world, are you not competent to judge trivial cases?'

The church is to act for God in settling its disputes by the exercise of godly judgment. The elders and shepherds who rule the flock are required from time to time to bring judgment so that issues are resolved. In these ways the church is being prepared and equipped to rule the universe under Christ when it has come to 'the full-grown man'.

The rights and wrongs

Let's imagine that a brother and I attend the same church and work as reps for the same firm. I find that all the reps, including this brother, claim full travelling expenses, whether they incur those expenses or not. It is financially profitable, but is it righteous?

I decide that it is dishonest. I have made a necessary and right judgment. So far so good. But if I now proceed to criticise my brother in the ears of others in the church, a right judgment has become a judgment of condemnation. What makes this judging wrong, while the other was quite right?

In the first place I have spoken behind his back before I have spoken to his face and heard what he has to say. The principle, 'Go and tell him his fault between you and him alone,' must apply here.

The fact that I did not do this would suggest that I am more ready to criticise my brother than to take steps to see him 'gained', as Jesus put it. My action is clearly not motivated by a desire for God's glory or the spiritual good of my brother, but for other reasons that we shall consider in a moment.

James, who tends to call a spade a spade, puts judging a brother in the same category as speaking evil of a brother (James 4:11). When we analyse what is so often the motivation, we see what he means.

Motivation is the key

This critical spirit that Scripture condemns does not come from above, but from beneath. Even when the judgment is correct — yes, that brother *may* be out for his own ends, or that sister *may* be jealous — it is nevertheless wrong because of its motivation.

Invariably it involves a subtle form of *self-aggrandisement.* The critic's words do not spring from heart concern, or he would have spoken to the person concerned first, or at least have talked to the Lord about it, which is seldom the case. Sometimes fear of the person criticised, or jealousy, lies behind the desire to put him down. But bchind the criticism is the clear implication, 'Of course, I myself would never be so unspiritual!'

Then there is *an accusing spirit* which needs to be traced back to its source. 'The devil' means 'the accuser of our brothers, who accuses them before our God day and night' (Revelation 12:10).

When Satan slandered Job before God the last thing he wanted was a change in Job for the better. When our words uncover our brother's nakedness, with no real desire for that nakedness to be spiritually covered, we are aligning ourselves with the accuser, being motivated by his spirit, and doing his work.

We are also guilty of *the sin of presumption.* We are assuming the role of God, the Judge of all — a role which he has not accorded to us. This leads us to pronounce judgment before we have heard the facts.

When a newspaper quoted a witness in a murder case that was due to come before the courts, implying that the accused was guilty, the editor found himself facing a charge of contempt of court. To pronounce judgment before the case was heard was to undermine the function and authority of the courts.

'Therefore do not pronounce judgment before the time, before the Lord comes' — even if we think we know the facts, we cannot discern motives. But the Lord, when he comes, 'will bring to light the things now hidden in darkness and will disclose the purposes [or motives] of the heart' (1 Corinthians 4:5 RSV).

To pronounce judgment when the Lord has not commissioned us to do so is to be guilty of contempt of the high court of heaven. Jesus said: 'With the judgment you pronounce you will be judged, and the measure you give will be the measure you get.'

A mature judgment

There are certain important principles we must bear in mind if we would develop a sound, mature judgment.

We must not trust our natural understanding. To make appraisals on the basis of what we see or hear is, in the words of Jesus, to 'judge after the flesh' or to 'judge according to appearance'.

'Trust in the Lord with all your heart, and do not rely on your own insight.' This is what Jesus did, and so the Spirit of the Lord rested on him, even the spirit of wisdom and understanding. 'He will not judge by what he sees with his eyes, or decide by what he hears with his ears; but with righteousness he will judge' (Isaiah 11:3-4).

We must learn *to set aside preconceptions and prejudices.* If we are to know a judgment that is swayed by the Spirit, we must learn to present that judgment to the Lord like a pair of even balances, so that he can put his finger on this side or that. How can he do this when we ourselves have a finger of prejudice or preference already swaying the balances?

There are other fingers that may come in to influence the balances. We must not be *enslaved by the opinions of others,* though always ready to give them a respectful hearing.

Of course, there are occasions when we must defer to the judgment of others, as in issues affecting the corporate life of the church, when we are required to submit to those who are over us in the Lord. But there are believers whose judgment is never allowed to mature because they are either shut up in an unhealthy way to one individual, or run from one to another to get an opinion, and end up in confusion. Let us give the Holy Spirit a chance to shape and influence our judgment.

This delicate operation of the Spirit is easily *affected by fear.*

Years ago I was discussing with a very able Bible teacher the subject of the baptism and gifts of the Spirit. I could tell that he was afraid of this whole realm of the Spirit's supernatural operation. I answered his questions and objections one by one. After an hour or more, he was asking the same questions he had asked at the beginning. I saw at once that he was inhibited by this fear. He could not make a proper judgment on what I was saying because he was scared of the possibility that I might be right.

Fitted to rule

As overcomers we are destined in the coming age to reign with Christ and to rule the nations. But the very essence of ruling is in the exercise of righteous judgment. God has given us this age of grace to prepare for it. If we cannot handle aright 'the pound' of responsibility entrusted to us now, who is going to ask us to rule over 'ten cities' in the coming age? If we cannot rightly judge the elementary matters of today, how shall we fare when it comes to judging the world and angels?

Let our faith rise to these staggering words of the great apostle: 'The spiritual man judges all things' (all, that is, that he is required to evaluate spiritually). He is not left to flounder in the dark. He has an anointing from the Holy One and he knows. His judgment is guided and enlightened by the Spirit.

Then he flings out that unanswered question of Isaiah, 'Who has known the mind of the Lord?' Who has *God's* evaluation, God's judgment of matters?

'No-one, surely,' would have been the answer of the Old Testament saints.

'Oh yes,' cries Paul, '*we* have, by the Spirit. As spiritual men we have the mind and judgment of Christ' (see 1 Corinthians 2:15-16).

The potential is all there. Let us see that we develop and use it.

Many streams or one river?

I saw a hill on which stood a cross silhouetted against the eastern sky.

On the side of the hill was a gushing spring whose waters flowed down the hillside to the valley below. It grew to a mountain torrent as it leapt and splashed its downward course, carving a bed for itself as it went.

By the time it had reached the plain it was a river, broad and deep. Large ships with cargoes for distant shores plied its waters. On the banks fishermen sorted their catches and spread their nets. The fields of this fertile plain were irrigated by its waters. Fruit-bearing trees along its banks sent their roots down into the well-watered ground.

This river, which flowed from the hill on which stood the cross, seemed unaffected by the prevailing seasons. Even in times of drought the river was full of water.

As I watched, enchanted by the sight, there came one who smote the river with his rod and divided it into several streams. Soon these in turn split into streamlets.

The waters that had been clear and sparkling when they first flowed from the hill on which stood the cross became muddied and polluted. Before, the current had been strong, now it was sluggish. Before, the river had had a single goal, now there were different streams flowing in as many different directions.

I was astonished and saddened by the change that overtook the scene. The whole plain seemed to be blighted. And I heard a voice that said, 'An enemy has done this.'

Then Another came who breathed on those divided waters. Immediately, the banks and strips of land that divided the streams began to dissolve into the waters as quickly as a sandcastle dissolves before the incoming tide.

As the land-strips were engulfed, stream embraced stream, laughing and leaping and jostling in the sheer joy of being together again. No longer were the waters slow and sluggish, but swift and strong. No longer were there streams each going their own way but one river headed for one goal, just as when it had first flowed from the hill on which stood the cross.

I opened my eyes and looked about me and discerned what God was doing throughout the earth. Then I knew that what I had seen was not a dream; it was true.

The supreme hope

I discovered it at the bottom of my desk drawer, an old penny.

How big and heavy it seemed compared with its modern equivalent, with the sovereign's head on one side and on the other Britannia, still brandishing her trident as she ruled the waves.

I reflected ruefully that as a boy of seven I used to feel as rich as a king to receive three such pennies for my weekly pocket-money. Just one was enough to purchase a whole handful of sweets. But now it would take the equivalent of two months' pocket-money to procure a packet of Polo mints. Such have been the ravages of inflation.

Much more serious is the debasing of spiritual currency, where we fail to give New Testament value to New Testament concepts.

One word which has suffered in this way is *hope*. Most often in everyday speech it conveys nothing more than positive thinking or human optimism: 'I hope it will be fine for the picnic.' When we transfer those ideas to 'hope' as the Bible speaks of it, we are guilty of devaluing our spiritual currency.

For most Christians, to compare hope with faith is like comparing my old penny piece with a current fifty-pence coin. They don't belong to the same league. Yet, in New Testament terms they are equivalent. Faith, hope and love are the three qualities that abide, when supernatural gifts pass away.

A key gospel word

Perhaps we have not noticed how often and in what key connections this word is used by the apostolic writers. They talk of 'the hope of the gospel', 'the hope of salvation', 'the hope of eternal life', 'the hope of righteousness', 'the hope of glory'.

The word expresses something of the character of our heavenly Father, for he is called 'the God of hope', and Christ's return is called 'the blessed hope'. Take away this hope of the future, says Paul, and limit our hope to this life only, and 'we are to be pitied more than all men.' Hope runs like a thread of gold through the gospel message.

'I think we have a very good man in Tom,' said a managing director about a new employee. 'I'm not saying anything to him, but I'm watching him very closely and, if he does well at his job, next year I intend to promote him.'

For this employee, the boss's intentions provided no stimulus to his efforts because he was ignorant of what was in mind. God could have designed our future inheritance on that basis, requiring us to be faithful simply out of a sense of duty, and without any further incentive. But he knew that with all the difficulty and discouragement we would have to face, we would need all the incentive that hope could provide.

We need motivating

'Hope springs eternal in the human breast,' and, 'While there's life there's hope.' So say the poets. But the truth is — as our prisons, hospitals and mental institutions confirm — there are large numbers in the world who live without hope. I say 'live', but 'exist' might be a better word.

On the other side, there are others who press on in the face of tremendous odds simply because of the hope that is still alive within them. Our Lord and Master knew that his disciples would have it tough, so he warned them of coming tribulation. Hope was to be the spiritual antidote, to prevent them being submerged in a sea of discouragement. We are born again, Peter tells us, 'into a living hope', so that we may rejoice despite having 'to suffer grief in all kinds of trials' (see 1 Peter 1:3-9).

There is another vital ministry served by hope. Have you not at times felt almost overwhelmed by all that you were required to do as a disciple of Christ? You are exhorted to read, meditate and study the Scriptures; to praise, pray and wait on God; to support and serve one another in practical ways; to be continually filled with the Spirit and exercise spiritual gifts; to know your calling and fulfil it in faith. And so one could go on. Every fresh exhortation you hear adds something else to the list.

You don't really need to be told more things to do, but how to find *motivation* to do the things you already know. Spiritual duties can become a bind and Scripture commands can become a burden if we have never been motivated.

Secret of faith and love

When I first left home for business in the Midlands I found lodgings with a farmer's widow. Her son had taken over the farm and he had a younger brother still at school. This lad of sixteen used to earn a little money by 'spudding thistles', that is, gouging them out of the meadows with a special tool. He hated the job, though he didn't mind the extra cash.

Then suddenly, to everybody's surprise, he became an enthusiastic thistle spudder! Without any prompting he was off every evening to a distant field close to one of the farm cottages, ostensibly hard at work. However, it was observed that as soon as he reached the spot a slim, attractive girl was seen leaving the cottage to join him! Attitudes are certainly transformed by an incentive.

If all our activity is to be worth anything to God it must be characterised by faith and love. Paul commends the Colossians for displaying 'the faith and love that *spring from the hope* that is stored up for you in heaven' (Colossians 1:5).

It is this hope that radically changes a person's attitudes, gives him new goals and ambitions, and causes him to relax his grasp on this world's goods. It sets eternity in his heart so that he ceases to be merely a man of time. He becomes strong in faith and love because eternity is now dominating his thinking.

Are you having battles in this area? Then the hope of your salvation has not yet gripped you.

What is the hope?

To the unbeliever, hope is nothing more than 'Pie in the sky when you die — if you're simple enough to believe in that kind of thing.'

The concept of many church-goers is little more. They have been taught to sing from Sunday school days, 'There is a happy land far, far, away.' But if the hope of the Christian is to be that powerful incentive to suffer and to serve that the Bible talks about, it must consist of something other than wearing a halo, sitting on a cloud and playing a harp.

When God broke into history in that great event of the incarnation, angelic choirs announced the fact. It is not surprising, therefore, that at the point when Christ's first advent terminated, angels appeared to announce the second. To an astonished band of disciples, gazing up into the sky where the figure of their loved master had just disappeared from view, they announced, *'This same Jesus,* who has been taken from you into heaven, *will come back in the same way you have seen him go* into heaven' (Acts 1:11).

This was only a fuller and more explicit statement of something that Jesus had told the disciples again and again while he was with them. The hope of the church is comprehended in that simple promise of Jesus: 'I will come again.'

Is it literal?

No serious student of the Bible could miss these oft-repeated references to Christ's coming again, but do they really refer to a literal, personal and visible coming of Christ?

Here it is important to recognise that not every reference to Christ's coming applies to what has come to be called 'The Second Advent'. Before the cross, Jesus told his disciples, 'In a little while you will see me no more, and then after a little while you will see me' (John 16:16), but the context shows that this coming was to be in the person of the Holy Spirit, and was fulfilled on the day of Pentecost.

There was an occasion when Jesus predicted, 'Some who are standing here will not taste death before they see the Son of Man coming in his kingdom' (Matthew 16:28). Whatever Jesus was referring to must have taken place in the lifetime of some of his hearers, and therefore could not refer to a coming that is still future.

The words of the angels, 'This same Jesus . . . will come back in the same way you have seen him go,' could hardly be more explicit. Just as he went up to heaven, personally, physically and visibly, so he would return.

'Look, he is coming with the clouds, and every eye will see him, even those who pierced him; and all the peoples of the earth will mourn because of him. So shall it be! Amen.' Here again is a promise that has yet to be fulfilled.

What will it mean?

Before 'the hope' can become the driving force in our lives that God intends it to be, we must understand its significance both for Christ and for us. First, it means *the hope of vindication* for the One whom the world condemned.

In 1894 Alfred Dreyfus, an officer in the French army, was found guilty by a military tribunal of divulging secrets to a foreign power. He was sentenced to life imprisonment on Devil's Island in French Guinea. Strenuous efforts were made on his behalf by those convinced of his innocence. It was not until 1906 that he was finally exonerated, reinstated in the army with the rank of Major, and made a Chevalier of the Legion of Honour.

The Son of God walked this earth unsoiled, the only one who

never forfeited the right to live, yet they impaled him on a Roman gibbet. They watched him being led, a condemned criminal, to the place of execution. There was no last-minute reprieve, no intervention of heaven's shining armies. In the awful loneliness of Golgotha he died, forsaken by God and abhorred by man. That was the last the world saw of him.

That was the end of Jesus of Nazareth — so they thought. Of course, we know that God raised him from the dead. But in his resurrection he did not appear to his enemies to confound them or to the world to prove his innocence; he only appeared to his disciples. He had been publicly condemned. He has yet to be publicly and universally vindicated.

Long before Christ's coming Scripture had predicted both his rejection and his vindication: 'The stone the builders rejected has become the capstone' (Psalm 118:22). His return in 'power and great glory' will be the final fulfilment of that prophecy.

'The Lord himself will come down from heaven, with a loud command, with the voice of the archangel and with the trumpet call of God.' There will be instant recognition and acknowledgement of who he is. Every eye shall see him, every knee bow to him, and every tongue confess that he is Lord.

He is coming back, Paul tells us, not to be glorified in any display of solitary grandeur, but in a way that will acknowledge and involve all those who sided with him and suffered with him in this day of his rejection (2 Thessalonians 1:6-10). If we have been identified with him in his suffering we shall share his glory and his vindication.

It also means *the hope of liberation* — both for us and for the whole universe.

The picture of a woman giving birth is how the Holy Spirit describes this: 'The whole creation has been groaning as in the pains of childbirth' (Romans 8:22). It is in a state of confinement from which it cannot escape, but 'in hope that [it] will be liberated from its bondage to decay and brought into the glorious freedom of the children of God'.

What we have tasted of liberty is only 'starters'. The main course is yet to come. We shall receive resurrection bodies, no longer subject to disease and death, and a freeing at last from the very presence of sin.

The creation itself will be brought into this freedom of God's children. That means that all the disastrous effects of man's fall will be erased. The curse will be removed. There will be a new heaven and a new earth free from the defilement of sin and in which righteousness dwells. There will be a universe enjoying the peace and harmony of God's government, just as he originally intended. Now we have to accept the fact of *limitation,* but in hope of that glorious day of *liberation.*

Finally, it means *the hope of reward.*

Some very spiritual people feel that we should serve God purely out of love, and without the incentive of a reward. Judging by the Scriptures they appear to be more spiritual than the Almighty himself! He has clearly presented 'reward' as a good and necessary spur to our spiritual endeavours. Paul, with the end of the race in sight, declared unashamedly that 'a crown of righteousness' awaited him. Elsewhere he exhorts us all, 'Run in such a way as to get the prize.'

What will these rewards be? Probably not material. The brief hints that Scripture gives us suggest that they will relate to the manifestation in the world to come of character, status and hence authority (Matthew 25:21; Luke 19:17; Revelation 19:7-8). How solemn to realise, 'What we weave in time we shall wear throughout eternity,' as someone has put it. What an incentive to faithfulness!

Hasten the day

For nearly two thousand years the appointed King has been awaiting with eager expectation the fulfilment of the hope. The Father has commanded him to sit at his right hand until his enemies become his footstool, to rule in the midst of his foes, promising that his sceptre will be sent forth from Zion (Psalm 110:1-2). In other words, he is to rule now through the church (Zion), and thus subjugate his foes. He is to sit until it happens. He cannot come again until it does.

It is true that the day of his coming is foreknown only by the Father. He has not even shared it with his Son. He does not want us to think in terms of a future day, unalterably fixed by divine fiat, but one which depends on the present fulfilment of his great kingdom programme.

How we live for God now is presented as hastening the fulfilment of our hope: 'You ought to live holy and godly lives as you look forward to the day of God and *speed its coming*' (2 Peter 3:11-12).

God's Word closes with that great affirmation of our heavenly Bridegroom: 'Yes, I am coming soon.' From earth comes the response of his waiting Bride: 'Amen. Come, Lord Jesus.'

The fulfilment does not simply depend on the promise of the Lord, but also on the response of the church. Let the hope of his return grip us and inspire us. Let us strive to be the generation that brings back the King.

It's time to get ready

The need of the hour, the voice of the prophet and the growing burden of prayer for the outpouring of the Holy Spirit are the clear indications today that God is preparing his people for something bigger than we have yet seen.

But will it come as a sovereign act of God? Or must we prepare for it?

One cannot read about past revivals without gaining the impression that God works when he will, where he will and through whom he will, without reference to man. God *is* sovereign and does as he pleases with the powers of heaven and with the peoples of the earth. Nor can anyone question the whys and wherefores of his working (Daniel 4:35).

This may tempt us to believe that we have little or no part to play, and that there is no way in which we can influence the situation. *That would be a big mistake.* We cannot so easily absolve ourselves of responsibility.

There are places in the Bible where God makes his powerful working contingent upon our obedience. God says, for example, '*If* my people, who are called by my name, will humble themselves and pray and seek my face and turn from their wicked ways, *then* will I hear from heaven and will forgive their sin and will heal their land' (2 Chronicles 7:14). In short, God says, 'If *you* will, then *I* will!'

God's chosen instrument

God seldom, if ever, acts directly in situations. In the heavenly realm he works through his angelic forces, even making use of the powers of darkness to accomplish his will. On earth he moves through human agency.

His purpose in this age is to take the gospel to the whole creation. How? Through his people. We are told to pray, 'Thy kingdom come.' But how will it happen? Through the body of Christ. *The church* is his chosen instrument for accomplishing *all* his purposes in this age, including revival.

It all began on the day of Pentecost. That great outpouring in Jerusalem was upon an assembled company who were destined to become the first church in history. Revival always begins, but does not end, with the people of God. Down the ages, the cry that has brought the visitation of the Spirit has always been, 'Will you not revive us again, that your people may rejoice in you?' (Psalm 85:6).

Though revival is an act of God that surpasses all human working, it is still true that the church is the channel through which that mighty power flows. This fact must challenge us with the question: *'Are we ready for such a visitation?'* Would it take us by surprise? Would it find us wholly unprepared?

Would the Almighty have to search elsewhere for a suitable instrument? No surgeon would ever operate with an unclean knife. No gifted craftsman would ever work with a blunted tool. No soldier would ever want to fight with a useless weapon.

Examine your attitudes

It is not the godless attitude of the world or even the opposition of the unseen powers of darkness that hinders the work of revival. It is primarily the attitudes of God's people.

History teaches us that wrong attitudes on the part of those who profess Christ's name may cause revival to be delayed, or if it comes, to bypass those who are not ready to receive it.

When the revival of 1904 swept through Wales, there were not only communities that knew a powerful visitation of the Spirit, with consequent transformation of the moral and spiritual life of the people, but there were other places that were left high and dry, completely untouched, even though they contained many who professed Christ's name.

Such were a people *un*willing in the day of his power. The revival came but they missed out. In a day of great gain, they were the losers.

Here are some prevalent attitudes among Christians that must change:

An attitude of complacency

'We have been filled with the Spirit, and so we already have revival,' some tell us.

Such a statement usually springs from a mixture of ignorance and complacency. If they really understood what revival was, they would not be so ready to make such a claim.

More serious is the attitude of self-satisfaction, that assumes they have arrived and that there can be nothing more to come. It smacks of the Christians in Laodicea, who described their spiritual state in the words, 'I am rich; I have acquired wealth and do not need a thing' (Revelation 3:17).

This attitude is the very contradiction of that hunger for God that so often characterises the period before revival comes. The antidote is to cry to God to show us ourselves as he sees us. Then to give us a vision of what he has in store for his people, which is 'immeasurably more than all we ask or imagine, according to his power at work within us'.

An attitude of resignation

'There's nothing we can do. It's all up to God.'

This makes the truth of the sovereignty of God an excuse for resigning oneself to the situation that exists. It's a kind of fatalism by which Christians escape from the responsibility that God has laid on them. It argues that if God wants to send revival, he will do so whether I prepare and pray, or whether I don't.

How does this differ from the case of the unprofitable servant in the parable, who buried his talent in the ground and whom his master described as 'a wicked, lazy servant' (Matthew 25:26)?

When we make use of a biblical concept such as the sovereignty of God to provide a cover for our own carelessness or indifference, we grieve the Holy Spirit and are a major blockage to the very thing we profess to believe in.

The state of the church, and our own spiritual condition in particular, are vital factors in the outpouring of the Spirit. Not until we repent of any spirit of complacency may we expect God to do this great thing among us.

Preconceived ideas and prejudices

These constitute another barrier. We think we are open to God, and so we are — *provided that he works within our terms of reference and does it according to our church traditions.*

We want to put God into a strait-jacket. We want him to put his seal of approval on our ecclesiastical set-up. This he is not willing to do. Any person who is not open to change is not open to God.

It is not that all change is right or for the better. But because God's people are not yet made perfect, either individually or corporately, and in some cases are far from it, change is a constant necessity. The man who opposes it, opposes the work of the Spirit and is a hindrance to revival.

What, then, are the characteristics of a church that is ready for such a visitation of the Spirit?

Prepared hearts

Whatever blessing a Christian may seek from God, whether it is baptism in the Spirit, victorious living, an effective prayer life or revival itself, the fundamental requirement is 'clean hands and a pure heart'. Only when we have these will we 'receive blessing from the Lord' (Psalm 24:4-5).

To suggest that God bestows his blessings willy-nilly, without regard to our spiritual state, would be to imply that God puts a premium on spiritual neglect and indifference. We have all surely discovered that this is not the case. There is a path of humility that we must tread. There is an opening of ourselves to God to be searched by his Spirit. There is a diligent dealing with God over those things which his light reveals. From this comes —

A new spirit of prayer

That first outpouring of the Spirit at Pentecost was born out of prevailing prayer. For ten days prior to the great event the disciples 'all joined together constantly in prayer, along with the women' (Acts 1:14).

What were they calling on God for during those days? It was surely the 'promise of the Father' to send the Holy Spirit. Note that they did not wait passively for this promise to be fulfilled. *They made the promise the ground of their pleading.* They sought God earnestly and continuously and in a spirit of faith for his promise to be fulfilled.

Many of us have received promises in a prophecy, or maybe in our reading of God's Word the Holy Spirit has made promises of revival come alive in our hearts. What are we doing about those promises? Are we twiddling our thumbs waiting for the thing to happen? Or are we responding as did those first Christians, letting heaven know that we are in earnest for a fulfilment of what God has said?

In recent times there has been evidence of a growing spirit of prayer among God's people, and much of this is focusing on the promise of revival. There is perhaps no more significant sign to show that revival is on the way. As Matthew Henry quaintly put it, 'When God intends great mercy for his people, he sets them a-praying.'

A body prepared

Does the corporate form and structure of the church influence in any way the outpouring of the Spirit?

Yes and no. There may be churches far removed from New Testament church life, bound by unscriptural traditions, who experience a mighty outpouring and are powerfully revived, despite the state of the 'wineskin'. But *if, subsequently, human traditions are not replaced by the lordship of the Spirit (2 Corinthians 3:17) among God's people, then those very traditions will reassert themselves and in due course suffocate the work of God.*

So, in the long term, the state of the church may greatly influence the permanent results of revival. Where there is unwillingness for adjustment and change, it is not long before the revival needs to be revived.

In Lewis, an island off the west coast of Scotland, an awakening took place in 1949 through the ministry of Duncan Campbell. At the time, communities were powerfully affected, with many turning to Christ. Among these were many called into full-time service, some at home and others overseas. But within a few years you could visit those communities and question whether they had ever known anything of revival. The iron hand of ecclesiasticism had reasserted itself.

'Lay people', as the 'established' church would call them, blessed and liberated through the movement of the Holy Spirit, could now no longer find an opening to use their gifts. What had before been tolerated and excused as the excitement of revivalism was now no longer permitted. Church life returned to its routine circuits, and the movement of the Spirit was quenched.

A suitable instrument

God always works through his people. The church is his agent for salvation and blessing. Jesus said to his disciples, 'You are the salt of the earth,' and, 'You are the light of the world.'

It is no different in this matter of revival. This activity of the Holy Spirit is the most powerful means by which God reaches the lost and answers the cry of our hearts, 'Thy kingdom come!' The church is still the channel of his working. Though the origin of the movement is clearly God, the state of the agent cannot be unimportant.

Revivals do not burn with a smokeless flame. Sometimes they even belch out acrid fumes! Some go off into extremes of fanaticism and error, even after beginning well. With other revivals, in spite of a seemingly powerful work of God, the results appear to be superficial and impermanent.

In all such cases we cannot attribute any blame to the divine Spirit. The negative influences must stem from the channel through which the Spirit was pleased to move. It was *the church* that fouled the waters. It was the church that took the thing off course. Because her spirituality was superficial, the results were correspondingly shallow.

The clarion call of the Holy Spirit to us at this time is 'Get ready!' In other words, the King is coming to display his majesty, power and glory, to make known to men and women the kind of God he is, so prepare for a day of visitation.

If we do not obey, revival may come and pass us by. Or we may be visited, only to be disappointed with the final results. Let not the day of God's power find us unprepared. It is time to get ready.

Discipleship

In the light of our Lord's commission, 'Go . . . disciple all nations,' to ask the question, 'Is discipling biblical?' is like asking the question, 'Is it biblical to preach the gospel?'

It was A.W. Tozer who reminded us that 'salvation and discipleship are so closely related as to be indivisible. They are not identical, but as with Siamese twins they are joined by a tie which can be severed only at the price of death'.

'Ah, but it's how you *do* your discipling that concerns us,' someone will be quick to reply.

Their fears lie in the realm of *authority*. In the controversy that surrounds the discipling or shepherding of believers, this is the root issue.

Every true shepherd has a rod and he cannot shepherd effectively without it. Discipling involves the exercise of spiritual authority, but is that authority used or abused? So often those who make charges of 'heavy shepherding' have never personally investigated the churches or fellowships they criticise.

I would like to remind them of Herbert Spencer's famous dictum: 'There is a principle that is a bar to all information, which is proof against all arguments, and which cannot fail to keep a man in everlasting ignorance: this principle is contempt prior to investigation.'

We do not ask our critics to take our word that we are not authoritarian or dictatorial, but that we seek to 'rule in the fear of God', as those who must give account. We invite them, if they are motivated with a genuine desire to know the truth, to come and see for themselves.

If they are people of wisdom and discernment they will quickly sense by the state of the sheep how the flock is being ruled, and whether the things they have heard are true.

A people cowed into submission by heavy-handed authority will be tense and fearful, with undercurrents of distrust and discontent, and their service will be marked by legalism. They will seldom have a life in God for themselves, and what is suppressed in the church will often erupt in the home.

If, however, they find a people rejoicing in God, secure under their shepherds, with a free spirit of worship and a hunger for spiritual things — if they find people who are growing in maturity as well as in numbers, with homes and families generally expressing the life and order of God's kingdom — then perhaps the discipling thing is not such a grievous error after all.

If they find that there are specific matters in which we are not spiritual or scriptural — and we do not claim that we have got it all right — then we are ready, very ready, to receive correction.

What we do reject, however, is the criticism of those who are not doing any effective discipling themselves. Charles Alexander, famous for the Alexander hymnbook, was accosted by a critic at the close of one of his meetings, who said, 'Mr Alexander, I don't like the way you do the work of God.'

'I don't know that I like it a great deal myself,' was the evangelist's disarming reply. 'Tell me, how do *you* do it?'

'Oh well,' expostulated the other, 'it's not my line, you know — I don't feel called . . . .'

'I see,' said the evangelist. 'Well, I think I like the way I do the work of God better than the way you don't.'

The rain is coming

Because God is both clothed in majesty and shrouded in mystery, there is something both majestic and mysterious about revival. It is a product of God that bears his own hallmark.

If we could come up with all the answers about it we should probably find ourselves disappointed and disillusioned. Both the majesty and the mystery provide a sense of wonder — and when we lose the sense of wonder we lose the sense of worship.

Though we are not to probe into the secret things that belong to God, we are to acquaint ourselves with the things that are revealed, and here there is much that relates to revival.

What is revival?

We must distinguish revival from evangelism. In evangelism man takes the initiative, though prompted by the Spirit, but in revival the initiative is God's. In the one the organisation is human. With the other it is divine.

A deep work in the hearts of Christians is implicit in revival but not necessarily in evangelism. Evangelism should be part of the continuous programme of the church, but revival is a thing of special times and seasons. Revival may break out in the course of evangelism, but in that case certain features will appear that are peculiar to revival, and others will disappear that are characteristic of evangelism.

Revival is more than big meetings and great excitement. It is more than a large harvest of converts. It is more than numbers of believers being revived and filled with the Holy Spirit. One may have any of these without revival, and yet revival includes them all.

Having prayed for a reviving of God's work, Habakkuk then describes what he sees in vision as the answer to his prayer: *'God came* . . . . His glory covered the heavens, and his praise filled the earth' (Habakkuk 3:2-3). Only two words, 'God came', but they furnish the best definition of revival I know. It is a visitation of God characterised by 'his glory', 'his praise' and 'his power'.

If God is omnipresent, what do we mean by a visitation of God? Though God *is* everywhere, he is in the hearts of those who love him in a way that he is not in the hearts of those who hate him. In heaven he 'dwells in light unapproachable' in a way that he could not dwell among even his greatest saints on earth. So when God visits his people he comes to them in a manifestation of his power and glory that is far beyond anything they normally experience.

It was for such a manifestation of God that Isaiah pleaded when he said: 'O that thou wouldst rend the heavens and come down, that the mountains might quake at thy presence . . . to make thy name known to thy adversaries, and that the nations might tremble at thy presence!' The New Testament counterpart of this is seen in the powerful outpourings of the Holy Spirit that commenced with Pentecost.

Revival can never be explained in terms of activity or organisation, personality or preaching. Whether or not these are involved they cannot account for the effects produced. It is something which has the stamp of God upon it, which even unbelievers are quick to recognise.

You cannot explain revival because you cannot explain God. 'The wind blows where it wills.' Though we may not understand 'the wind', at least we can learn to work with it.

His will or ours?

How does revival come? Is it a sovereign act of God without regard to any human factors? Or does it come inevitably when God finds some people who will obey certain laws or fulfil certain conditions?

Certainly it is a sovereign act of God, but that is not to say that it is exercised without regard to the spiritual response of his people. God's sovereignty (or ability to do what he wills) is subordinate to his character of holiness and love. Because he is a moral Being and has constituted man a moral being, he cannot act without reference to his moral principles. For example, even a sovereign God cannot forgive the unrepentant!

Most of God's promises are contingent on the response of his people. He says, 'If my people . . . will . . . then will I . . .' (2 Chronicles 7:14).

There are many examples in the history of revivals of God waiting for his people to come into line, though they were but a handful, before he poured out his Spirit. There are also cases where pride and carnal ambition among his people brought a promising revival to a halt. That we are commanded not to 'quench the Spirit' proves that it is possible to do just that.

On the other hand, it is equally erroneous to emphasise human responsibility without recognising the mystery of God's sovereignty. Because a group of God's people fulfil certain conditions does not mean that a powerful visitation of the Spirit will inevitably and immediately follow. The 'when', 'where' and 'how' of God's answer is bound up in the mystery of his will that he may not always reveal.

The initiative in revival is always God's. Having taken all known factors into account, we are still left with the element of mystery, and are compelled to exclaim with Paul, 'How unsearchable are his judgments and how inscrutable his ways!'

All the principles of revival are seen in that first great outpouring of the Spirit. 'When the day of Pentecost had come' suggests the sovereign timing of God, fulfilling the prophetic meaning of Pentecost as the Feast of Firstfruits (compare 'the firstfruits of the Spirit' — Romans 8:23), just as the offering up of the Lamb of God had to take place fifty days earlier, at the Feast of the Passover.

'They were all together in one place' points to what had been going on in the hearts of the waiting disciples, to bring them to a place of unity and readiness for the promise of the Father. Thus Scripture presents both divine sovereignty and human responsibility side by side without any attempt to reconcile them. The truth is in both. When we hold them in tension we hold the truth in balance.

That fallow ground

'Break up your fallow ground,' cries the prophet Hosea, 'for it is time to seek the Lord, that he may come and rain salvation upon you' (Hosea 10:12 RSV). Here, as in many other passages of scripture, the visitation of the Spirit is pictured as a heavy downpour of rain, and the prophet is telling us to prepare for it.

That we are called to make preparation does not mean that we are taking things out of the sovereign hands of God, or that we are trying to 'buy' this blessing, any more than when we emphasise in the gospel the need for people to repent and believe we are implying that they can thereby earn salvation.

'Break up the fallow ground' speaks of heart-preparation. 'It is time to seek the Lord until . . .' suggests praying through. Fallow ground is not desert that has never been cultivated. Nor is it necessarily land that has returned to desert through being abandoned. So God is not here addressing either the unbeliever or the backslider. Fallow ground may be quite fertile, but it is uncultivated and so idle.

We are 'God's field' (1 Corinthians 3:9), but are we lying fallow? Fallow ground is *hard*. That is why it needs to be broken up. Hardness does not mean that we have denied the faith or fallen into gross sin. We may hold the right doctrines. We may be receiving the finest teaching, but like the wayside ground of the parable, the seed never penetrates. Hardness means that though we may be hearing ministry, we are not hearing God. 'Today, when you hear his voice, do not harden your hearts.'

Once the fallow ground in our lives has been broken up and the spiritual weeds eliminated we shall begin to hear what God is saying. He longs to share his secrets with us. He longs to whisper in our ear what he purposes to do. 'Behold, the former things have come to pass,' he says, 'and new things I now declare; before they spring forth I tell you of them.' This is not to tickle our imagination or to satisfy our curiosity, but that our hearts may become thirsty, and faith may be born in them for the answer.

It is invariably the case that in the period preceding a visitation of the Spirit there were those who had prepared their hearts and, like 'the watchmen of the walls', were on the spiritual lookout to see what God would show them. The situation may have been grim, but they had heard God. The secret of the Lord is with them. God has not envisioned them simply that they might have hope, but that they might have an indispensable part in the bringing in of what God has purposed.

Praying through

Fallow ground holds its moisture. There is an air of lethargy and self-sufficiency about it. But once the soil has been opened up by the plough it becomes thirsty, as though silently pleading for rain.

Once we have fully allowed the Holy Spirit to open up our hearts, we, too, will begin to experience a holy dissatisfaction with the status quo, and a deep longing will take possession of us for the visitation of the Spirit.

'It is time to seek the Lord until he comes and rains righteousness upon us.' Deep heart-preparation is essential to produce this kind of prevailing prayer. But when it comes you may be sure that the rain will come sooner or later.

'Ask the Lord for rain in the time of the latter rain [which precedes the harvest] . . . . He will give them showers of rain' (Zechariah 10:1 RAV). As we have already said, revival is a thing of times and seasons. When is the time to seek it?

'In the time of the latter rain,' and only God is able to show us when that is. The timings of the Lord are all-important. In years gone by I have well-nigh prayed myself to a standstill, without seeing the answer from heaven, either through preconceived ideas about the answer, or through trying to compel God to move before his time had come.

We must know that the prayer burden is God-imposed and not self-imposed, then he will sustain it. (It is hard work when we try to keep going what we ourselves have initiated.) Such praying will not leave us in a state of nervous exhaustion, nor will it be a strain to go on believing. We will be continually buoyed up by God-given hope.

If the limit of our vision is successful evangelism or the blessings of the charismatic movement, or even what we are now experiencing of kingdom life, then the Lord is wanting to whisper in our ear, 'You will see greater things than these.'

The fewness of God's people in a fast-expanding world, the strength of the adversary, the shortness of the time, all call for the greatest outpouring the world has ever seen. Let God open our hearts to receive the vision of it and then, as he puts the burden for it on our hearts, let us plead the promises and pray through.

Fit to fight

The church is not a holy club but a fighting unit.

Every Christian is called to military service. There are no exemptions. The battle is clearly hotting up, and it is time to face the question, 'Are we fit to fight?'

God redeemed his people Israel with a view to their possessing the land of Canaan, and they could only do that by driving out the enemy. So, early on in their travels, God instructed Moses to take a census of the people. 'Every man of Israel, twenty years of age and over, fit to bear arms, must be registered by you and Aaron and assigned to his fighting station' (Numbers 1:3 Jerusalem Bible).

Notice that this registration involved 'every man'. It was a total call-up of those who were 'twenty years of age and over'. There had to be a measure of maturity. And then each had to be 'fit to bear arms'.

If we want our names to appear on the register of those who count in the battle of the ages, we must make sure that we are fit to fight, so that God can assign us to our fighting stations.

I am writing in the midst of the Falkland Islands crisis, with a British naval task-force steaming towards the southern Atlantic. Great alarm and concern have been expressed that our sailors, soldiers and airmen are going into a potential battle zone. Someone could actually get hurt!

That's because everybody is thinking in the context of peace and not of war. Soldiers do not exist to occupy comfortable barracks, grace regimental parade grounds, fire weapons on firing ranges or participate in military manoeuvres. They exist to fight. That's how we all thought during World War Two, for our very existence was at stake.

As believers, we are involved in a deadly conflict until the final battle is won. There will be no taking of the kingdom without intensive warfare. There needs to be a radical change of attitude and outlook in this whole matter. The cost of war is very great. It cannot be won without self-sacrifice. God cannot place our names on that register of those available for battle unless we have got through on this issue.

When a nation is being threatened, no political leader can call that nation to war without first preparing the minds of the people to face the issue. The very first arming must be the arming of the mind of the nation, because war involves sacrifice and suffering (1 Peter 4:1).

Internal battles

No nation is fit to fight if torn with internal dissension. The pressing need would be to solve its internal wrangles. The slogan holds true, 'United we stand, divided we fall.'

All this is true of us individually as God's children. If we are preoccupied in dealing with the internal enemy, 'the flesh' (or self-life), we cannot deal with the external enemy, the devil.

After their departure from Egypt, Israel could have reached Canaan in days had they taken the direct route. Why did they not do so? Because Canaan meant conflict, and God knew they were not yet fit to fight (Exodus 13:17). Two years later they were still not ready. When the spies brought the news of giants and fortified cities they were ready to turn tail and return to Egypt.

What was the matter with Israel? They were too busy fighting their internal battles to be able to cope with the real enemy. Apart from a one-off conflict with the Amalekites, there was no war during their wilderness wanderings, but plenty of in-fighting. There was rebellion against Moses' leadership, grumblings against God, discontent with God's provision and lusting for the flesh-pots of Egypt. So God had to let a whole generation go, and start all over again.

Are the battles you are now fighting internal ones? Is it a battle with that uncontrollable temper? That rebellious attitude? That proud spirit? That unruly tongue? That undisciplined appetite? If this is where your conflict lies, you are not yet fit to fight the Lord's battles. You are too busy fighting battles of your own.

The apostle James speaks about this when he says, 'What causes fights and quarrels among you? Don't they come from *your desires that battle within you?*' (James 4:1). Similarly Peter: 'Dear friends, I urge you, as aliens and strangers in the world, to abstain from sinful desires, which war against your soul' (1 Peter 2:11).

If this is where we are, we are still immature and need to grow up spiritually. We need to seek grace from God to get through on these issues. Until then he cannot use us in the battle. We would be much too vulnerable and would soon become casualties. We must seek him for real resolution in these areas of internal conflict.

Can you hold ground?

When we read Paul's classic passage on spiritual warfare in Ephesians 6:10-18, one interesting point clearly emerges. The apostle is not dealing with offensive but defensive warfare.

All the armour is defensive, and even the sword is to enable us to hold our ground. We are to 'stand against the devil's schemes' (v11). Paul tells us to 'put on the full armour of God so that . . . you may be able to stand your ground, and after you have done everything, to stand. Stand firm then'.

Learning how to stand, how to hold ground, is the first great lesson in spiritual warfare. It's the secret of victory. But what does this mean? And how do we do it? Have we not to win the ground before we can hold it?

The marvellous truth is that the ground has already been won — by Christ! At the outset of the Ephesian epistle Paul informs us that God 'has blessed us in the heavenly realms [that's where all the fighting takes place] with every spiritual blessing in Christ' (1:3). The ground is what we have inherited 'in Christ'. He has won it for us. We know it is ours because he has given us the title deed in the form of specific promises.

The first challenge to Israel on entering Canaan was the strongly fortified city of Jericho. Did you know it was won by defensive warfare?

Before the battle God told Joshua, 'See, I have delivered Jericho into your hands' (Joshua 6:2). Now, it didn't look that way to Joshua. Those frowning walls still looked impregnable. But God's word had dramatically changed the ground of battle. It was now being fought in the realm of faith. Would Joshua act as though he believed God, or would he believe his physical senses?

God's promise had in fact given him a change of position. Physically, Joshua was still outside the city, but by faith he was now in occupation. God's promise had given him ground to stand on. The walls, however, did not immediately collapse, so he had a fight on his hands, but it was the fight of faith.

For a further seven days they behaved as though they believed God, and disbelieved what the situation appeared to be. They held the ground that the promise of God had given them, until the shout of faith brought the walls crashing down.

It works today

Some years before the outbreak of the charismatic movement, God spoke to me about my need of the Holy Spirit. There was no-one I knew to whom I could turn for counsel or prayer, but after seeking God and searching the Scriptures, there came a point when God spoke a promise to my heart.

I declared to my wife, 'My dear, I've got it!'

So I had — in the realm of faith. I never again asked God to baptise me in his Spirit. For two days I thanked him that the experience was mine, and then one memorable spring morning the Comforter came. Hallelujah!

You are praying for an unconverted family, for the supply of some need, or perhaps the solution to some intractable problem. God speaks a promise into your heart and the battleground immediately changes. You believe God and confess that what he says is true.

You cannot see that there is any change, but change there certainly is. You are winning the battle by holding the ground, by fending off with the shield of faith all the fiery darts of doubt that the devil hurls against you. Then, in due course, the promise is fulfilled and the victory is won.

King David and one of his mighty men were once surrounded by a horde of Philistines. 'They took their stand in the middle of the field. They defended it and struck the Philistines down, *and the Lord brought about a great victory'* (1 Chronicles 11:14).

When the testing time is prolonged, we are tempted to lose heart, feeling that nothing is happening, and the devil does his best to persuade us that this is the case. But here is where resolute faith is needed. We need to say, 'By the grace of God, I will not give up.'

Using the sword

No soldier is fit to fight if he does not know how to use the weapon with which he has been issued.

'The sword of the Spirit which is the word of God' is introduced in the context of the believer's defensive equipment. Each piece is tremendously important. We should study the equipment and by faith appropriate it piece by piece. But for now let's focus on the sword of the Spirit.

'Word of God' here does not simply refer to the Bible. You

may have a Bible, read it, know it and discuss it, but still never wield the sword. 'Word of God' here (Greek *rhema*) means 'utterance of God'. To wield the sword means to utter the word in faith, just as Jesus did when attacked by Satan. Three times he declared, 'It is written . . .' and eventually Satan retreated in disorder.

Don't just read the word, or think the word, but speak it out. Be ready to quote such scriptures as: 'The reason the Son of God appeared was to destroy the devil's works' (1 John 3:8); 'I have given you authority . . . to overcome all the power of the enemy' (Luke 10:19); 'Resist the devil, and he will flee from you' (James 4:7).

It is good to know them by heart, and to have them at the ready. But remember, no scripture is an abracadabra. It is only the truth *spoken in faith* that is effective.

Most important is our confession of the promise that God has given us for the current situation. This is an indispensable weapon in the accomplishing of the victory.

Psalm 2 reveals that this is the weapon used by Christ when he was installed as king on Zion's hill. He says, 'I will proclaim the decree of the Lord: He said to me, "You are my Son; today I have become your Father. Ask of me, and I will make the nations your inheritance, the ends of the earth your possession."' So our Lord Jesus is taking the kingdom by declaring what the Father has decreed to him.

We must learn to do the same.

The church — a fighting unit

When Jesus introduced to his disciples for the first time the concept of this new community which he called 'the church', he made it clear in the minds of his disciples that this was not to be considered a religious club, but rather a fighting unit.

The context was one of spiritual conflict. 'I will build my church, and the gates of Hades will not overcome it. I will give you the keys of the kingdom of heaven; whatever you bind on earth will be bound in heaven, and whatever you loose on earth will be loosed in heaven' (Matthew 16:18-19). So the first thing Jesus said about his church was that it would triumph, and then, as though explaining how, he spoke of binding and loosing.

The only other time Jesus specifically mentioned the church was two chapters later, when teaching them how to handle an insubmissive brother in the congregation. He said, 'I tell you the truth, whatever you bind on earth will be bound in heaven, and whatever you loose on earth will be loosed in heaven. Again, I tell you that if two of you on earth agree about anything you ask for, it will be done for you by my Father in heaven. For where two or three come together in my name, there am I with them' (Matthew 18:18-20).

The only two occasions when Jesus spoke of the church, and each time he went on to speak of her authority to bind and loose! How significant, and yet how little attention the church has paid to this authority invested in her. Her neglect has resulted in weakness and ineffectiveness.

What is the significance of this word of Jesus, and how do we fulfil it?

Binding and loosing

Jesus preceded the promise to Peter about binding and loosing by saying, 'I will give you the keys of the kingdom of heaven.' This is generally taken to mean that Peter unlocked the kingdom to the Jews on the day of Pentecost, and unlocked the kingdom to the Gentiles in the house of Cornelius.

This is no doubt true, but keys are used for locking as well as unlocking, shutting up as well as opening. Also, since authority to bind and loose is given to the church in general two chapters later, there is no reason to think that the keys are the sole property of Peter.

Binding is the authority God has given us to deal with all activity that is opposed to the kingdom of God. This may be the direct activity of Satan, or it may be the activity of those who are inadvertently doing his work. By this means the church can neutralise, or counter, some activity of the enemy.

Jesus shed light on this when he pointed out that no-one could enter a strong man's house and carry off his possessions without first binding the strong man (Matthew 12:29). From the context it is clear that Jesus was talking about Satan and his kingdom.

Judicially, this binding was done by our Lord Jesus at the cross. It was there that, by death, he destroyed the one who had the power of death, that is, the devil (Hebrews 2:14). It was there that he 'disarmed the powers and authorities' (Colossians 2:15). But this *has to be made effective* in every situation we face. When we do this by the prayer of faith, we are binding Satan in that situation.

One has seen the immediate effect of God's people binding and loosing in a variety of situations. Quietening satanically-inspired disturbances in meetings. Rendering ineffective the disruptive influence of demonised people who were not ready or willing for deliverance. Thwarting the schemes of ungodly men who were opposing the work of God.

Psalm 2 envisages God's people throughout the earth so using their authority that even kings and rulers of the earth gang up in their futile attempts to resist their binding influence (v2-3). This is how the saints take the kingdom, making the nations Christ's inheritance and the ends of the earth his possession (v8). Binding is the key to bringing in the kingdom (see also Psalm 149:6-9).

It is time that the legislative assemblies of the world felt the impact of believers praying in faith. Our authority may extend even to blocking unrighteous bills that ungodly men are seeking to make law, or compelling unrighteous laws to be removed from the statute books.

Learning how to loose

Jesus not only spoke about binding the strong man, but added that this was with a view to spoiling his goods. There are countless men and women who are prisoners in the strong man's house, waiting to be released. We all know of those, believers or unbelievers, who give evidence of being bound by Satan. Where Satan and his agents are active, there is a challenge to bind. Where Satan and his agents are binding individuals or situations, there is a challenge to loose.

One day in the synagogue, Jesus freed a woman from a spirit of infirmity which was affecting her physically, preventing her from standing up straight. He described her as 'a daughter of Abraham, whom Satan has kept bound for eighteen long years' (Luke 13:16). There are many sons and daughters of Abraham today who are bound, some physically, others by a spirit of pride, jealousy or fear. We have authority to set them free.

There are numerous situations in which the work of God has come to a standstill, locked up by the activity of Satan. We are not called to cry over spilt milk, or wring our hands in despair. Jesus says to us, 'Have I not given you the keys of the kingdom? Why do you not use them?'

We don't need to have a lot of experience or a great deal of maturity, but we do need to have faith in the promise of God and in the authority that the Lord has given us. Then we can turn the key and unlock the situation. Then we can speak the word of faith: 'Be loosed in Jesus' name.'

Now is the time to start

Many of us may feel we are not yet ready to be involved in warfare of this kind. But we can begin to flex our muscles.

There are many situations right on our doorsteps calling for warfare. But David could not have ventured forth to tackle Goliath if he had not first proved himself by dealing with a lion and a bear that attacked his flock. The young shepherd boy on the Bethlehem hills could hardly have realised that by slinging his stone and wielding his club he was taking the first steps to the throne, and the bringing in of God's kingdom in his day.

It is as we, too, prove God in the small situations that he can entrust us with the greater. As we take our stand, even the gates of Hades will not be able to prevail against us.

In a pill-box at Passchendaele, on its reoccupation by allied troops during World War One, the following *Special Orders to Number 1 Section* were found, dated 13 March 1918:

1. The position will be held and the section will remain here until relieved.

2. The enemy cannot be allowed to interfere with this programme.

3. If the section cannot remain here alive, it will remain here dead, but in any case it will remain here.

4. Should any man, through shell shock or such cause, attempt to surrender, he will stay here — dead.

5. Should all the guns be blown out, the section will use Mills grenades and other novelties.

6. Finally the position, as stated, will be held.

T.P. Bethune, Lieut.
Officer Commanding No. 1 Section

That's the kind of resolution we need in the Spirit!

Personal fitness checklist

What about you? Are you fit to fight? Check yourself out against this personal fitness checklist:

1. Have you dealt with those longstanding minor conflicts? Don't give God any rest until they are resolved.

2. Have you dealt with any areas of unconfessed sin or constant weakness in your life? These make you vulnerable to Satan and must be dealt with before you are fit to fight.

3. Have you specifically told God you want to be on his fighting register, that you are available to be taught and trained?

4. Have you discovered other believers who will join you in a prayer cell? Using your weapons is so much easier when you fight together, shoulder to shoulder.

5. Are you making a practice of waiting on God to receive his directions (Romans 8:26-27)?

6. Have you found fellow-Christians who will join you in learning to bind and loose? Whatever you agree on earth, that shall be done in heaven.

7. Are you prepared, when God gives you a promise about a situation, to confess it and hold on to it until it is fulfilled?

The grand finale

What is the meaning of history? Where is it all heading? How will it wind up?

To come up with any answers we must first ask an even more fundamental question: Why did God ever create the universe in the first place? Once we find an answer to that, we possess the key to history and the understanding of the grand finale.

It was in 1946 that I found myself in Perugia, a university town in Italy. The army had arranged various courses to prepare us soldiers for our return to 'Civvy Street'. With a call of God on my life for full-time service, there was little that offered me any help, except a course for Church of England ordinands on New Testament Greek and philosophy!

I recall the philosophy instructor making this point: 'I don't know why God ever created the world. I would have thought that he would be happy to spend eternity contemplating his own perfection.'

Why, then, *did* he create the world? Does Scripture suggest a reason?

A love gift

'God is love' is a profound statement. It teaches us that the Godhead could never have been a single being, as the Jehovah's Witnesses teach, for love cannot exist in isolation. If God was love before anything else existed, then God must have included a Lover, a Beloved and a Spirit of love. There we have the Trinity. The old divines used to say, 'God is a sweet society.'

It was out of this fellowship that 'God said, "Let us make . . ."'. Concerning the creation of the universe Scripture says, 'All things were created by [Christ] and for him' (Colossians 1:16). It was all to do with this love relationship within the Godhead: 'The Father loves the Son and has placed everything in his hands' (John 3:35). So the universe was in fact the Father's love-gift to the Son.

As possessor of heaven and earth, God appointed his Son as

his heir, before anything existed to be inherited. He then used him to bring the universe into being. Jesus is the 'heir apparent' to the throne of the universe.

The grand design of history is to bring God's Son into the possession of his inheritance.

In his matchless wisdom God has chosen to involve redeemed men and women in the accomplishing of this great end. Not only are they to have a vital role in this but they are actually to share in the heavenly inheritance itself! The church is to be glorified with Christ, to sit down with him on his throne, to be heirs of God and joint heirs with Christ.

It was this 'secret wisdom . . . that God destined for our glory before time began' that drew from Paul this exclamation: ' "No eye has seen, no ear has heard, no mind has conceived what God has prepared for those who love him" — but God has revealed it to us by his Spirit' (1 Corinthians 2:9-10).

The counter move

The fulfilment of this great purpose was not to be an easy path. There were factors in the situation that were antagonistic to God's purpose.

From the angelic hierarchy rose one who had determined in his heart to challenge that purpose. Pride, jealousy and greed drove him to aspire to the position that was destined for the Son of God. In the temptation of the wilderness he tried to strike a deal. Showing our Lord all the kingdoms of the world in a moment of time, Satan promised that all should be his if only he would acknowledge Satan as supreme by bowing down and worshipping him.

The conflict of the ages involves this same challenge of the usurper to the rightful heir. There is no question that God could, if he chose, put paid to Satan forthwith. Satan is a creature, God is the Creator. Satan's powers are finite, God's are infinite. The usurper is neither omnipotent, omniscient nor omnipresent.

Instead, God has *chosen to wage war through his church.* By this means he is preparing them for the throne, and equipping them to enter into his inheritance.

Path to maturity

Spiritual conflict is the indispensable means by which we are purified and matured. The French laughed at Napoleon's youthfulness when he sought to obtain a seat in the Chamber of Deputies. He replied, 'Men mature quickly on the battlefield and, gentlemen, it is from the battlefield that I have come.' He won his seat.

The call of Christ is not simply to forgiveness and eternal life; it is a call to conflict. Christianity is not merely receiving the gift of eternal life, with soldiering as an optional extra. They come together as part of one package deal. When Ezekiel saw in his vision the dry bones coming to life, they stood up on their feet and were at once 'a vast army'. When we are raised to life in Christ we are thereby constituted Christ's soldiers.

In the Olivet discourse, Jesus instructed his disciples on the events leading up to his return in glory. He indicated that the conflict would inevitably intensify. This is confirmed by the book of Revelation that describes the great finale. It is a book full of warfare, but the final issue is never in doubt!

All things in Christ

The doctrine of 'all things' (referring to the whole universe) is one of the great themes of Scripture. Not only did Christ create the universe in the beginning, and continues to sustain it by his word of power, but it also exists *for him.* He is now waiting at the Father's right hand, to see his enemies become his footstool and the kingdoms of this world become his rightful possession.

God's purposes for this world are Christ-centred. Any prophetic scheme must be judged on this issue. Docs it focus on the glorification of God's Son? 'The testimony of Jesus is the spirit of prophecy' (Revelation 19:10).

All the tragic effects of sin, alienation, disunity and defilement will be dealt with by Christ in this great work of restoration, when God brings all things in heaven and earth together under his headship.

Some have bent Scripture to teach that all men and women will ultimately be reconciled to God. Some have even asserted that the devil himself will eventually be saved! But we must not isolate the scriptures that, at first sight, may seem to point that way from other important statements in the Bible. There *is* a lake of fire, there *is* a second death, there *is* a going away into eternal punishment. No wishful thinking must allow us to dilute these clear and solemn facts.

Doom or boom?

Some prophetic students see no hope for this age short of the return of Christ. They major on scriptures concerning 'things waxing worse and worse', iniquity abounding and the love of many growing cold. The return of Christ is presented as our only hope. It is viewed as a gigantic rescue operation to save us from final eclipse.

This would mean failure to have accomplished what Christ commanded. How could the return of our Lord be the glorious consummation of victory that the New Testament presents it to be, if those are to be the circumstances of his return? We are to be the salt of the earth and the light of the world. He commissioned us to preach the gospel to the whole of creation and to disciple all nations. If the church fails, how can any of us receive his 'Well done, good and faithful servant'?

Others see the predictions of failure and apostasy as having been already fulfilled, and predict a time of great advance and expansion. The light will grow brighter until it gradually gives way to a golden millennial age. Christ will then return to a world over which Christianity has largely prevailed.

I do not believe that either of these views represents the true picture.

Without doubt, world conditions will deteriorate, there will be a falling-away on the part of many and there will be an increase in the conflict between light and darkness. But as the darkness gets deeper the light will get brighter! Doom and boom are not mutually exclusive. They will go on side by side.

The greatest chapters of church history have yet to be written, the greatest harvest has yet to be reaped. In spite of opposition and persecution, the story of the early church was one of success. But Jesus did not describe that successful beginning as the harvest. The harvest, he said, was 'the end of the age'. James likewise speaks in terms of the coming of the Lord being the harvest-time (James 5:7-8). But he reminds us that this cannot come without the early and the late rains.

Early and late rains

These two rains were essential for the harvest in Israel. The early rain enabled the farmer to plough and sow, while the late rain swelled the grain in preparation for harvest.

Both are necessary also for the *spiritual* harvest. If the outpourings of the Spirit at the start of the age were the early rains, the late rains, with their heavier downpour, are still to come before the final harvest.

'This gospel of the kingdom will be preached in the whole world as a testimony to all nations, and then the end will come' (Matthew 24:14). These words were spoken by Jesus in the context of end-time events. Though the gospel was to be preached throughout the age, the final phase before his return will be one of intense world evangelism.

The expression 'the gospel of the kingdom' means that this end-time evangelism will be in word, in work and in wonder, just as it was in the time of Christ and the early church. 'This salvation, which was first announced by the Lord, was confirmed to us by those who heard him. God also testified to it by signs, wonders and various miracles, and gifts of the Holy Spirit distributed according to his will' (Hebrews 2:3-4).

The church moving in fulness

This period of intense evangelism will spring out of the Gentile church coming to full maturity, which Paul describes as 'the fulness of the Gentiles' (Romans 11:25-26 NASB). The spiritual hardening of the Jews will then be removed, 'And thus all Israel will be saved' (for I take this to refer to natural Israel). This in turn will trigger off greater blessing for the world than was received through Israel's original rejection of the gospel (Romans 11:12, 15).

This will no doubt be the great final harvest and a fitting climax to the age, preparing the bride for the return of the Bridegroom. For him as well as for us it will be a day of exultant joy, when he is 'glorified in his holy people and . . . marvelled at among all those who have believed' (2 Thessalonians 1:10). How could that be true if he was not returning for a triumphant church that had accomplished its world mission?

We all need an encouraging and inspiring view of the ultimate triumph of the kingdom of God. This is the coming of the kingdom for which Jesus taught us to pray. The return of our Lord is not to bring about a victory that the church failed to accomplish. He returns for an *overcoming* church, eagerly awaiting his return, and thus he will crown the victory which has always been his people's portion.

God's ecumenical movement

By 'ecumenical movement' I am not referring to the World Council of Churches! Their effort to get it together is based on misconceptions both as to what a Christian is and to what the church is. They look for the lowest common denominator of truth that the churches can agree upon. It is a confederation of weakness and compromise and can never produce 'the unity of the faith'.

The fact remains, however, that 'the church of the firstborn, whose names are written in heaven', do need to get it together. How often we have looked at situations and said, 'If only God's people in that place could flow together, what an impact they could make.'

Since Jesus prayed 'that they may all be one', unity is clearly on God's programme and must find fulfilment. Scripture reveals that God has 'a plan for the fulness of time, to unite all things in [Christ], things in heaven and things on earth' (Ephesians 1:10 RSV). This must include the unifying of the body of Christ, though it is much bigger than that. It is a unifying of the universe that will take place at 'the fulness of time'.

Just as the 'restoration of all things', while it awaits that great day (Acts 3:21 NASB), is a process already begun, so it is with the bringing together of all things, which must begin with Christ's segmented body. This is a vital part of restoration. It will mean reaching out beyond our own circle and will be more costly than fellowshipping only with those who see it our way.

How can we do it? For a start we can recognise humbly that neither we nor our fellowship have yet arrived. We must keep an open heart to all in the body of Christ, however limited their vision. *He* does. The greater their need, the greater the reason for not withholding fellowship. If there is withdrawal, let it not be of our making. And let us be open to try again. Think of those who persevered with *us*.

We must be prepared to receive as well as to give. That could lead to some surprises. To get on with our vision and 'let the devil take the hindermost' is not the spirit of Christ. Let us pray that we may feel for the body of Christ as he feels. Then, as its true unity emerges and God's great purpose comes to fruition, to the grand finale, our joy will be unrestrained.

On the path to victory

Though it is true that the ultimate victory for the church awaits Christ's return, there are many who still view this event as a kind of 'Dunkirk rescue' operation for God's people.

It is as though the church is a boxer losing every round. Then in the last few seconds of the final round, when he is pinned to the ropes and being slaughtered by his opponent, the referee puts a stop to the fight, not by holding up the attacker's hand in victory, but by delivering him a knock-out blow!

Christ's return, according to this view, is to achieve in a moment what the church failed to achieve in two millennia — and this despite Christ's victory over Satan at the cross, despite his present possession of all authority in heaven and on earth, despite his commissioning of the church to disciple all nations and his pouring out of the Spirit to make it possible.

From such a view of the progress (?) of the kingdom, may the Lord deliver us.

The whole Book is a message of victory. God is winning every round of the contest and has every phase of the fight under control. Christ's return should be seen as the climax of *a process of victory* in which we are involved right now. 'The Lamb will overcome them because he is King of kings and lord of Lords — and with him will be his called, chosen and faithful followers' (Revelation 17:14).

The ultimate victory of the church has its beginnings in the victory of the individual believer. Too many have the idea that one born of God has to struggle and strive, fast and pray before he can mature into being an overcomer. But John tells us that everyone born of God is an overcomer (1 John 5:4-5).

At the new birth we receive overcoming life. We are born to conquer just as certainly as the fish of the sea are born to swim. The believer who walks in victory is demonstrating to unseen powers the victory of Christ. He is contributing to Satan's final overthrow.

Of course, conquering personal temptation is only the

beginning. That is defensive victory and God wants to move us to the offensive. This means that we not only overcome Satan's attacks on us, but that we actually invade the house of 'the strong man', tie him up and walk off with the plunder.

There is a conquest of the gospel involved here. It was demonstrated in measure in the early church, as for example in Ephesus, where 'the word of the Lord grew and prevailed mightily'.

There is to be a hurling down of Satan to bring in the power and the rule of God, and Scripture shows that this is effected, not by the second advent of Christ, but by 'our brothers' who 'overcame [their accuser] by the blood of the Lamb and by the word of their testimony' (Revelation 12:11).

Brothers and sister, that means *us!*

THE BEST IN CHRISTIAN READING

Other good books from Harvestime

Stay or Move?

Church loyalty

by Tony Ling

Should I leave the Anglicans for the Baptists if I change my views on baptism? Should I move to one of the 'newer' churches just because I like its worship and preaching? Is faithfulness more important than success? Is it selfish to put my own needs before those of the people who rely on me in my present church?

Tony Ling gives no pat answers to these and similar topical questions but offers pointers to help make the vital decision: Should I stay or move?

ISBN 0 944714 63 4 £3.95

Apostles Today

edited by David Matthew

Few topics are of greater interest today. Questions abound: Didn't apostleship die out with the Twelve? Or, if there are apostles today, how do we recognise them? Is an apostle the apex of a pyramid of authority? What about apostolic teams — how are they formed and how do they operate?

This compilation of writings by a variety of authors — including the late Arthur Wallis — tackle these and related questions. Many of the writers are recognised as apostles by a growing number of Christians in Britain today.

ISBN 0 947714 58 8 £3.25

Revelation

Meaningful mysteries for today

by Terry Brooks

Beasts, horns and crowns. Trumpets, seals and plagues. Angels, thrones and bowls of wrath. John's language seems foreign to readers in our scientific age. Some have given up any attempt to understand it. Others have fallen into bitter controversy about details of interpretation, especially over chapter 20's millennium. But for the simple-hearted, Revelation is a book of comfort and encouragement second to none.

Terry Brooks' treatment is for the ordinary Christian reader who wants to catch the spirit of John's great vision.

ISBN 0 947714 29 4 £3.75

The Covenant Meal

Meaningful communion

by David Matthew

This fascinating new look at the Lord's Supper draws its title — and its emphasis — from Jesus' words: 'This is my blood of the covenant.'

David Matthew addresses thorny issues like the polarised Roman Catholic and protestant interpretations of 'This is my body . . . blood' and Paul's puzzling statement about sickness and death through unworthy participation. But the book's main burden is a plea for a new closeness between Christians within the new covenant, expressed in the 'holy informality' of the covenant meal.

ISBN 0 947714 51 0 £3.75

These books are available from leading Christian bookstores, or, in case of difficulty, direct from: Harvestime, 12a North Parade, Bradford, West Yorkshire BD1 3HT. For all orders under £10 please add 75p postage and packing.